Computers at Work

Edited by
John O. E. Clark B.Sc., A.R.I.C.

illustrated by Whitecroft Designs Limited

Hamlyn
London · New York · Sydney · Toronto

FOREWORD

This book does not describe how a computer works. It does not go into computer theory nor does it give a complete account of all the various uses to which a computer can be put. Instead, we have tried to select interesting applications of computers which illustrate their versatility in terms of what they can be made to do in activities that affect ordinary people and their work – or will do so in the near future.

To assemble the material we have drawn on many sources, from university and medical research to commercial undertakings specializing in computer technology. I would like especially to acknowledge the contributions made by D. Cheesman, J. Hawgood, and P. Endersby, and to thank the various companies who made available material for illustrations.

John O. E. Clark.

Published by The Hamlyn Publishing Group Limited
London · New York · Sydney · Toronto
Astronaut House, Feltham, Middlesex, England

Copyright © The Hamlyn Publishing Group Limited 1969
3rd impression (revised) published in paperback 1979
Hardback edition published 1979
ISBN 0 600 32204 1

Phototypeset by BAS Printers Limited, Wallop, Hampshire
Colour separations by Schwitter Limited, Zurich
Printed in Spain by Mateu Cromo, Madrid

CONTENTS

4   Introduction
6   The need for planning
12   Aircraft and navigation
18   Money
24   Traffic control
35   Power stations
46   Printing
52   Airlines
79   Weather forecasts
84   Medical automation
95   Computers for making computers
101   Information retrieval
113   Steel works
120   Message switching
130   Police records of cars
136   Design automation
144   Freight terminals
152   Conclusion
156   Books to read
157   Index

INTRODUCTION

The computer industry is one of the most rapidly growing branches of modern technology. It has expanded from the experimental stage to mass production in only fifteen years. Most new developments in electronics are immediately adopted by the industry, giving more powerful and versatile computers. Whether small or large, there are two basic types of computers: digital and analog.

A digital computer uses electronic circuits to perform accurate calculations at extremely high speeds. The information fed into the machine, called the *input,* is generally converted on special typewriters into punched cards or paper tapes, and there are other types of input which are described later in this book. The apparatus that converts the information into a form that can be handled by the computer is called a card reader or a tape reader.

An analog computer is used for applications in which the input information is varying with time. Practical problems can be simulated by apparatus that generates varying voltages which the machine can handle and analyse.

The way a computer approaches a given problem is determined by the way in which it is prepared for its task. The preparation includes supplying the machine with complete instructions and these constitute the computer *program.* Facts for future reference, called *data,* are retained along with the program in the computer's store, or memory, and the machine is designed in such a way that all the information in the store is available immediately it is required by the program. The store is supplemented by a magnetic drum, disk, or tape on which information, in the form of electrical impulses, is stored almost as sounds are 'stored' on the magnetic tape of a domestic tape recorder.

Once a calculation has been completed, the computer delivers the answer as *output* which may take the form of a teleprinter or a line printer (which produce 'hard-copy'), a television screen on which the answer is displayed, or an apparatus producing punched cards, paper tape, or magnetic tape. A teleprinter types one letter at a time, and a *line printer* produces answers quickly, one complete line at a time.

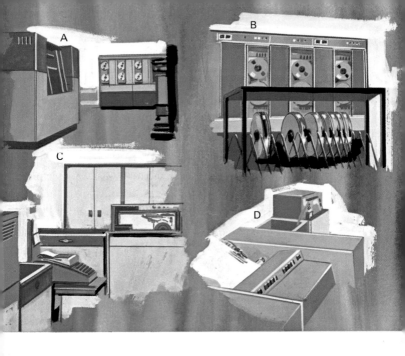

Computer installation (A), magnetic tapes for storing data (B), keyboard input for typing data (C), tape reader and printout (D).

All the various units from which a computer system is built are collectively referred to as *hardware*. The ancillary services available to the users of a computer – such as a library of standard programs, and so on – are called *software*.

A common requirement of many industrial and commercial organizations is to know what is the best way, in terms of either cost or time taken, to tackle a job that involves several stages. Some stages may depend on others, some take longer, and some require more people to do them. Traditionally, this is the function of planning and we shall consider the part a computer can play at the very beginning of a project. It can examine all the various alternate and interconnected tasks involved from the start of an undertaking to its completion. It can determine the sequence that will give the shortest possible overall time. It can find the *critical path*.

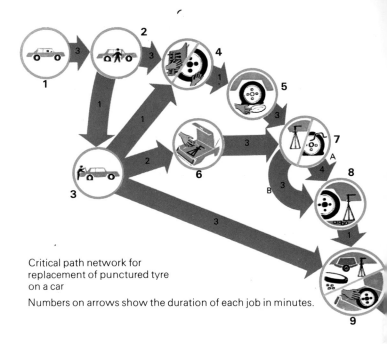

Critical path network for
replacement of punctured tyre
on a car

Numbers on arrows show the duration of each job in minutes.

THE NEED FOR PLANNING

The critical path method can be used to plan, schedule and
supervise any project. On highly complicated and involved
operations, the executives can call on a computer to determine the critical path. The sort of information required is the
precise timing of the various activities. For instance, when
will design specifications be needed? When must certain
materials be ordered? Which activities will be affected by a
delay and for how long?

Definition of terms

Each task or job is called an *activity* and is represented on a
critical path *network* as an arrow (the length and direction of
the arrow is not necessarily significant). The *duration* of each
activity is the time taken to complete it and is given in
appropriate units such as minutes, shifts, days, weeks, and so

on. The start and finish of each activity is called an *event*. The events on a network are numbered in series and represented by a circle. An activity is identified in terms of its event numbers and its duration.

As a simple example of critical path analysis, we shall consider the activities involved in changing a punctured tyre on a car. The illustration shows the activities, with their durations, from the time the driver notices a flat tyre until he has changed the wheel and driven off. The ways in which this whole operation can be planned and carried out depend on the number of people available. If there are at least two people in the car, jobs two and three (unlocking the boot and removing the tools) can go on at the same time as job four (checking the flat tyre), but they must all be completed before anyone can start work on job five because the tools are needed to remove the hub cap.

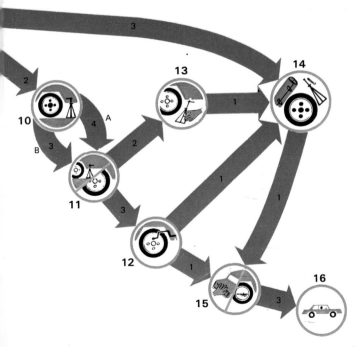

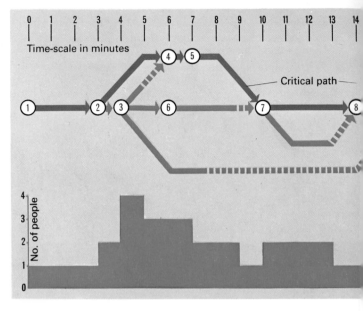

Critical path network at earliest stage of planning with block diagram of resource usage

The diagram overleaf showed the critical path network with each event numbered and the duration of each activity. When two activities start and finish with the same events, the activities are lettered A and B (as in 7–8A–8B). The network shows the correct logical sequence for all the activities.

The critical path

Often different paths between the same two events take different times. But all the activities are necessary to the whole project; all the paths taking the *longest* times linked together form the critical path. This path determines the shortest possible total time for the project. These factors are illustrated by drawing the network.

The solid lines on the time-scale network diagram (on this page) represent activities and span the correct lengths for the times taken. Dotted lines represent slack time on an activity

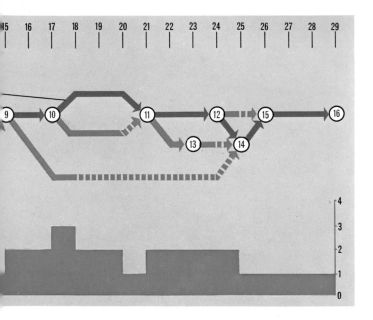

when an operator has nothing to do and is waiting for another activity to be completed. Slack time is known as *float* and it occurs on the shorter of alternative paths between two events. The critical path runs from the start event to the end event without float. Our example takes twenty-nine minutes.

Resource scheduling

Most activities involve a piece of equipment, raw materials, or manpower, and these factors are called *resources*. For the tyre-changing project, we may assume that the required resources are one person employed for the duration of each activity. The way the resources are used may be illustrated by a *histogram*, which is a chart showing the resources (number of people) occupied for each time interval (from minute to minute). For example, four people are required during the fifth minute of the histogram on this page.

9

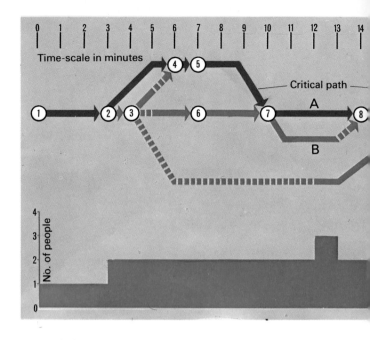

Critical path network after resource scheduling with block diagram of resource usage

We can re-schedule our example by assuming that there are only two people in the car and that we want to change the tyre as quickly as possible. By moving some of the activities within float, it is possible to make use of a person (resource) who would otherwise be idle. The resulting resource-usage histogram is much more level and nearer to the ideal form. The process of moving activities within their floats and trying to make the best use of resources is called *resource scheduling* (or resource levelling). The new network is logically the same as the first and the project still takes twenty-nine minutes, but some activities start later.

Using a computer
The network for changing a tyre was chosen to illustrate a technique. It is small, involving only twenty-three activities,

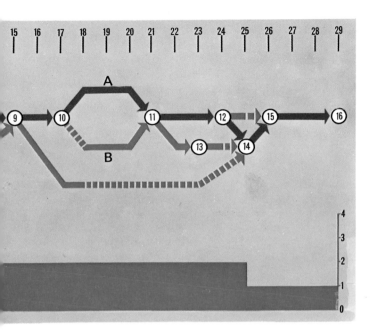

and may easily be processed by hand. But when a network consists of several thousand activities with perhaps up to fifty resources, it is an enormous task to discover the critical path. And there must be no errors in logic, in drawing the network, and in calculating the critical path.

The method of finding the critical path is called *time analysis* and involves computations for all activities of the earliest and latest start, earliest and latest finish, and total float. Activities with zero total float all lie on the critical path.

The repetitive process of resource scheduling and time analysis can be carried out extremely quickly by a computer and any volume of information can be produced. Almost inevitably some operations on a project fall behind schedule. A computer can show that it is necessary to expedite only certain critical activities to bring the project back on schedule.

Satellite in orbit

AIRCRAFT AND NAVIGATION

While an aircraft is in flight, the conditions round it may change rapidly. A human pilot has only limited reactions to deal with these continuously changing situations, which may include sudden pressure changes, variations in wind speed and direction, and so on. Ever since World War I, machines to help control an aircraft in the air have been getting more and more complicated as flying speeds and safety requirements have increased. By World War II, analog computers (then called 'automatic pilots') were being used to control an

Navigation by computer and satellite

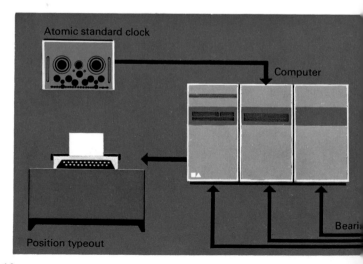

Atomic standard clock

Computer

Position typeout

Beari

aircraft in level flight. These devices were not electronic; they used gears, cams, and levers to carry out the mathematical calculations involved.

By the 1950s, sophisticated electronic analog computers were being used for many purposes in aircraft – for navigational calculations and control, automatic pilots, flying controls, and engine controls. The need for absolute safety demanded that these analog devices be separate, so that the failure of one central device could not lead to complete loss of control. Even some of the individual control devices were duplicated and triplicated, when safety required it.

As flying speeds increase, control decisions must be taken more quickly. But analog computers cannot analyse data; they can only react to the physical conditions inside and outside the aircraft and indicate something *after* it has actually happened. For example, an analog computer measuring true airspeed can indicate an increase in speed only after the increase has occurred. Also, an analog device cannot decide between two courses of action. This inability to decide has meant that large aircraft have to have a flight

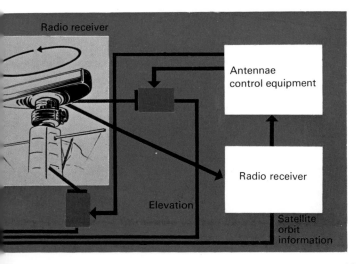

Radio receiver

Antennae
control equipment

Radio receiver

Elevation

Satellite
orbit
information

engineer, who reads and analyses all the data from these control systems and makes overall decisions. All the masses of data are used for calculations made by the navigator or the engineer, but for the answers to be meaningful, the calculations should be made thousands of times every second.

It is here that the high-speed airborne digital computer is used. Vast quantities of analog data can be collected from all over the aircraft and changed into digital form by high-speed analog-to-digital converters. The digital computer can scan all these inputs very rapidly and use the data it obtains to perform calculations, make decisions, and either present the final data to a member of the crew or convert the digital signals back into analog form to be used to control some internal function of the aircraft.

At first, digital computers were far too large to be of any use in aircraft as they required inputs and outputs in the form of paper tape or card punchers and readers which have bulky electronics. Today, the introduction of integrated circuits and miniature thin-film memories has made in-flight

Ground control room

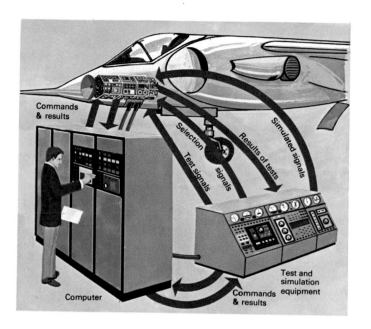

Automatic checking-out of radar equipment. In more sophisticated equipment the checkout of each piece of equipment in the aircraft would be performed by the equipment itself. The computer would then examine each piece of equipment to see if it were 'good' or 'bad'.

computers a reality. The computer's functions can be changed merely by changing the program, so that the same computer can be used for various applications in different aircraft. These devices are now being made so small, that whole computer systems can be duplicated to give increased safety.

Automatic checking of rockets and aircraft

Supersonic aircraft, missiles, and rockets for space experiments have become so overwhelmingly complex that it would take human operators days, even weeks, to check all the functions of the equipment involved. An automatic checkout computer can analyse a complete system, such as a supersonic fighter, very rapidly. It checks each function in sequence and does not make errors that a tired or distracted human operator may make. And the programs of such computers can easily be changed so that they *check-out* other pieces of equipment.

The largest checkout equipment developed so far is the system for the United States' Apollo moon project, which uses 125 separate computers. At the other end of the scale, air forces and airlines are using portable equipment that can be wheeled out to the aircraft and plugged in to check rapidly all the functions of the aircraft before its next flight.

Special techniques have to be used in such systems to enable some 'active' measurements to be made. For example, a human operator may have to break an electric circuit at some point to measure the current flowing along a wire. A computer cannot do this, so that special devices have to be included in the design of the various circuits so that current and other active measurements can be made without breaking or changing the circuits.

One future development may be to include a checkout computer in the system being checked, so that should a malfunction occur, the checkout computer will indicate the position of the fault. Many systems of this sort from several missiles or aircraft could all be connected to an external computer, which would check the checking computers!

Navigation by computer and satellite

One of the latest ways of accurately pinpointing the position of a ship anywhere on the oceans of the world uses navigational satellites. If three satellites orbit the earth in different orbits at the same height and speed, they can be arranged in such a way that at least one satellite can be 'seen' by radio from any point on the earth's surface.

Radio signals from each of the satellites can be received on a ship, together with the bearing and elevation of the nearest satellite's position. The signal received will identify the satellite as one, two, or three. An atomic clock feeds time signals, plus the satellite information, into a computer.

The time signal from the atomic clock is used to sample the input data at a fixed instant in time. The exact position of the satellite is then determined from the time and the computer's

stored details of the satellite orbits. Having determined the position of the satellite, the computer uses the elevation and bearing of the received signals to calculate the precise position of the ship on the surface of the earth, with reference to the position of the satellite.

This process can be a continuous one, the clock being used to sample the satellite signals every few minutes and producing a typeout of the ship's position. The great advantage of this system is that the information about position is continuous and automatic and that it produces accurate results in any weather conditions.

A similar arrangement may be used to navigate steerable space capsules orbiting the earth or journeying to the moon. In this case, the position of the computer (on earth) is accurately known and signals are sent to the satellite to alter its course when necessary.

From several minutes before blast-off, the final count-down and actual firing of space rockets are controlled by computers. Later the computer orders the firing of second and third stage rockets, automatically applying any necessary corrections to the rocket's course.

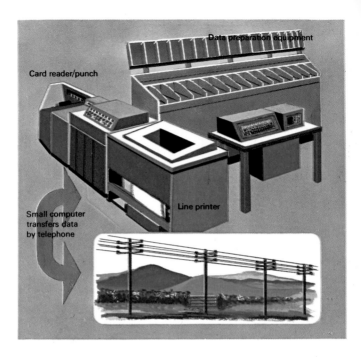

Data terminal for banks

MONEY

Routine clerical tasks were among the first jobs to be given to
computers, mainly because such tasks occur in large numbers
and are of a standard type. Typical applications include
banking, stock exchanges, stores holding and stock keeping,
payrolls, and accounting in insurance offices and finance
companies. So diverse are all these applications, that most
computer manufacturers have a 'library' of programs
for basic tasks which they combine to suit each customer's
requirements.

Stock exchanges

The data system for a stock exchange begins at a stock-
broker's office where a customer decides to buy or sell

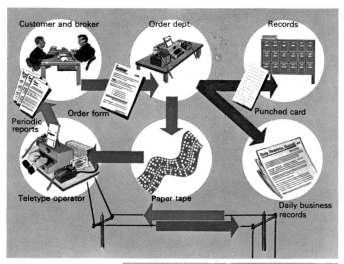

Customer and broker · Order dept. · Records

Order form · Punched card

Periodic reports · Teletype operator · Paper tape · Daily business records

Control of stockbroking

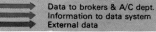

Data to brokers & A/C dept.
Information to data system
External data

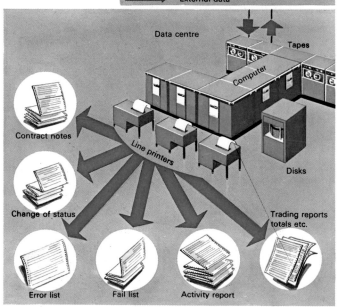

Data centre · Tapes

Computer

Line printers · Disks

Contract notes

Change of status

Error list · Fail list · Activity report · Trading reports totals etc.

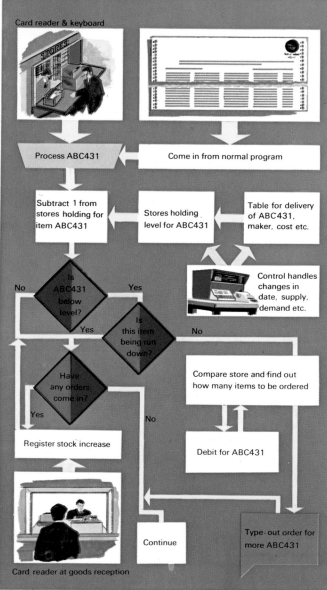

Card reader & keyboard

Process ABC431 ← Come in from normal program

Subtract 1 from stores holding for item ABC431 ← Stores holding level for ABC431 ← Table for delivery of ABC431, maker, cost etc.

Control handles changes in date, supply, demand etc.

Is ABC431 below level? — No / Yes

Is this item being run down? — Yes / No

Have any orders come in? — Yes / No

Compare store and find out how many items to be ordered

Register stock increase

Debit for ABC431

Continue

Type-out order for more ABC431

Card reader at goods reception

20

securities of some sort. The broker makes out a 'buy' or 'sell' order form, detailing the transaction that has just taken place. The office then transfers this data onto punched cards for storage, and at the same time types the transaction onto a daily list of business. Punching the cards also results in a punched tape output. At the end of the day, a length of punched tape detailing all the day's transactions is available and this is fed via teletype to a central stock exchange data processing centre. At the data centre, the transaction is credited or debited to the customer's account, and the securities sent for transfer and delivery to the customer. After a day's trading, the computer analyses all the transactions made and prepares statements for each broker.

A 'fail' list is prepared which details all failures to deliver, collect, or pay for transactions. This list is always complete in that a transaction will not be removed from the list until it has been settled correctly, and it therefore contains transactions from many dates.

An activity report is also prepared which shows the trading for each firm, detailing all securities that have changed hands. An error list is prepared which shows all errors of accounting or transferring that have not been rectified. Any new customer or change of status of customer is *typed-out* on a 'change of status' card, copies of which are sent to relevant brokers.

Stores holding using a computer

In very large manufacturing industries, it is uneconomic to store large quantities of component parts which represent idle money and wasted storage space. But if stores holdings are too low, the stores may run out of a component before the delivery of the next consignment. The stores 'holding level' must be maintained at such a quantity that normal numbers can be drawn out of stores, and when a certain minimum level is reached more of the components can be ordered.

One method of computerizing stores holdings is to use a punched card system for checking items in and out of the stores. Each item that enters is allocated a punched card detailing its part number, and this is read into the computer

Flow chart for computerized stores

by a 'one shot' card reader at the goods reception point. The code number is stored in a computer which keeps a record of the number of these items held in stock.

When someone draws this item from the stores, the storeman removes it from the shelves and passes the punched card through a card reader. The computer immediately subtracts one from the total of these items held in stock, and then examines the total to see if it has fallen below the minimum stock level. If the minimum holding has been reached, the computer again refers to its files to see if this item is being 'run down', when no re-ordering would be needed. Otherwise the item, its supplier, and the quantities needed are typed-out and the cost debited to the stores holding account.

Banking

The type of computer system used for banking purposes is very similar to that described for stock exchanges. One rapidly developing aspect of banking systems is the use of data links from branches to a data centre.

Each bank in the system has a *data terminal* connected over telephone lines to the central computer. The day's business (account numbers and sums of money) is continuously sent to the main centre which calculates a statement of the bank's balance at the end of the day. A person's credit at any branch can be checked by interrogating the main system, and so it should soon be possible to cash cheques immediately at any branch. When the central computer has a full page of transactions on a person's account, it sends all the data over the link to be *printed-out* at the data terminal.

Such systems will enable quick turnround of banking transactions. For example, if someone who has an account in Bristol cashes a cheque in Liverpool, his Bristol account can be brought up to date the same day.

Banks of different companies having similar systems may eventually all be 'on-line' to computer-controlled clearing houses. As a result, the flow of money from an account in one bank to an account in another will take minutes rather than days, and cheques can be 'cleared' almost immediately.

Country-wide data system for banks

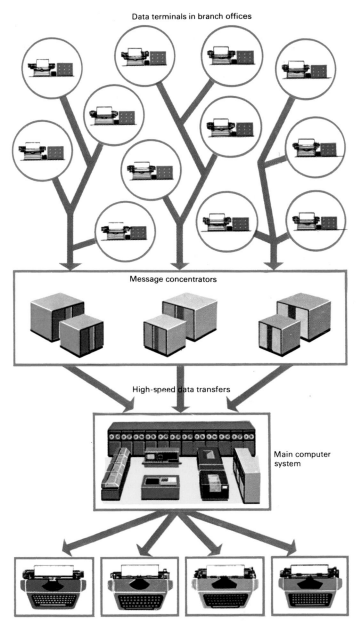

Data terminals in branch offices

Message concentrators

High-speed data transfers

Main computer system

Office typewriters

Pressure pads in the road activate the central control computer which controls traffic lights via a time switch. Operators at the central control check traffic with television cameras.

TRAFFIC CONTROL

Town traffic

In most towns, the two main ways of controlling traffic at a junction use either policemen or conventional traffic lights. The main difference between these methods is that a police-man can judge the number of vehicles approaching from various directions and whether or not there are any traffic jams on the next sections of road, and traffic lights, of course, cannot.

Computer control of all the traffic lights at a group of junctions can combine much of the flexibility of the police-man at an individual crossroads with the ability to react to the overall traffic situation in the whole of the area controlled.

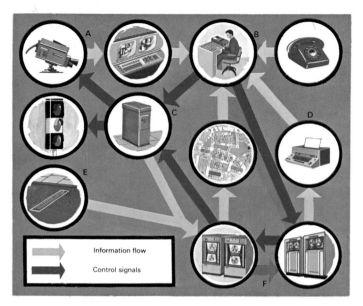

System of computer-controlled traffic lights (*above*): televisual message (A), operator (B), switch-box (C), monitor printer (D), vehicle detector (E), message and control computers (F). The control centre (*below*).

The traffic lights at all the junctions can be set to give the best traffic flow in all directions.

The computer can take into account minute by minute changes at all points, and make special arrangements in emergencies for the rapid passage of ambulances, fire-engines, and so on, by setting all the lights green on the route required. The best route can be selected according to the known traffic situations on the alternative routes.

The system consists of a central control computer fed with information on traffic flow by pressure pads (or other types of traffic detectors) at many points in the area covered. This computer sends messages to work the traffic lights at all the controlled junctions according to the overall picture of the situation and a set of built-in rules (the program). There are a number of complications introduced by the large number of different messages coming and going – there could be hundreds of traffic lights and thousands of vehicles in the area being controlled – but the basic idea is quite simple.

The equipment in the street has three functions to perform: detecting vehicles, controlling the traffic flow, and monitoring the resulting situation. There are generally separate systems to perform the three functions, only two of them being connected to the central computer.

Detection of vehicles is carried out by devices sunk in the road surface at various places, not only at street junctions. There are two main types, either of which produce an electrical signal when a vehicle passes over. One type is the familiar pressure pad which reacts to a heavy weight; the other type is an induction-loop detector which reacts to a moving metal object. The signals produced by either type are sent along a cable to the control centre. We shall assume that there is a separate cable for each detector, although there are ways of letting them share cables.

Controlling the traffic flow is the function of ordinary traffic lights, but the switch-box which changes the signals has a timing mechanism that can be altered by the central computer. When the lights change, the switch-box informs the control centre so the state of the lights is always known.

Part of system (one-way only) showing placing of equipment

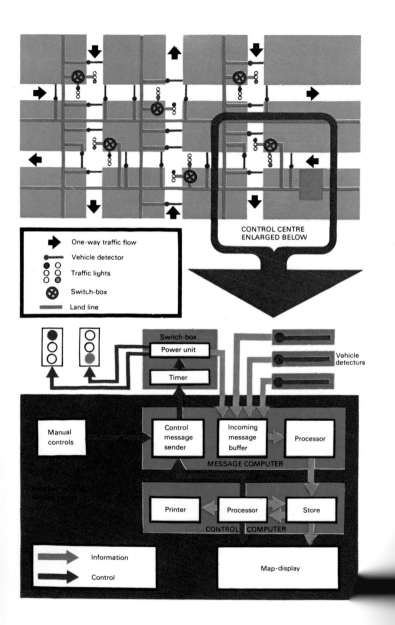

CONTROL CENTRE ENLARGED BELOW

One-way traffic flow
Vehicle detector
Traffic lights
Switch-box
Land line

Switch-box
Power unit
Timer

Vehicle detectors

Manual controls

Control message sender

Incoming message buffer

Processor

MESSAGE COMPUTER

Printer

Processor

Store

CONTROL COMPUTER

Map-display

Information
Control

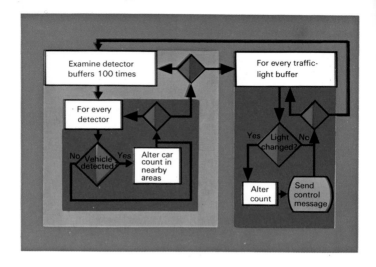

Flow chart for message computer

Monitoring may be done by closed-circuit television cameras which can be adjusted in direction and focus by the human controllers at the centre who use them to observe the traffic situation, particularly in case of emergencies or blockages. This system is independent of the computer, and need not always be provided.

The equipment at the control centre consists of two computers, a display showing the traffic densities and traffic-light settings, and the television monitor screens. The operators will have control consoles to override the computer in case of emergency or breakdown, and telephone and radio communications with the police and other services. Both computers generally have duplicates to allow for failures and routine maintenance.

A message computer is needed in addition to the control computer because of the large number of messages coming into the centre (one signal is produced every time a vehicle passes a detector). If there are 1,000 detectors and each street carries 1,000 vehicles an hour, there will be nearly 300 vehicle-detection messages reaching the centre every

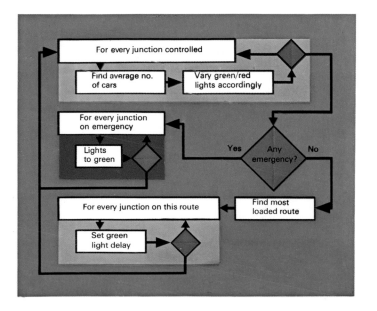

Flow chart for control computer

second, as well as the traffic-light-change messages. The control computer would have no time to perform its main function if it had to deal with all these messages, so they are handled by the message computer. Each detector feeds its signal into a different *buffer register* in the message computer, and its processor examines each buffer in turn (perhaps 100 times a second) to see whether a signal has been received since the last examination a hundredth of a second before. Whenever it finds that a signal has been received, this information is passed to the control computer, to up-date the traffic-situation record held in its store. The message computer will also handle outgoing messages to the traffic-light timing mechanisms, sending a message to the switch-box at a road junction when a signal reporting a light-change is received from that junction.

The control computer keeps in its main store a record of the traffic density in each road section in the area. It also records the current situation and timer-settings for each set of traffic lights. These records are shown on a map-display for the operators. Also in the main store there is the control program which adjusts the timer-settings to produce the greatest traffic flow on the most popular routes, which vary from time to time. The program instructs the computer to examine the traffic flows approaching each road junction in turn, to compute the number of vehicles approaching from each direction, and to set the green/red traffic-light time ratio taking account of the information received.

The quickest way to the seaside

In controlling traffic at road junctions, no attempt is made by the computer to arrange which route the traffic should follow; it is assumed that the drivers know where they wish to go

Diagram showing the layout of an advisory system for drivers

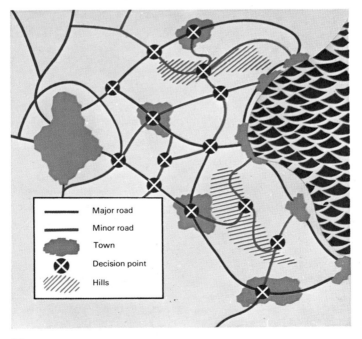

	Major road
	Minor road
	Town
	Decision point
	Hills

The computer display tells the driver approximately how long it would take him to get to the seaside by taking one of the three possible ways at this junction. Using this information, he can make his own decision which way to go – or turn back !

and which is the best way. The computer merely tries to help them to get there, using that route, as quickly as possible. But the information stored in the computer about the traffic situation throughout the controlled area can enable it to work out the best route between any two given points.

Let us consider that many thousands of cars from a certain large town wish to travel to the coast, and that there are a number of alternative routes with interconnections at various points. The computer system is set up so that displays at the *decision points,* where alternative routes diverge, give the drivers enough information about the congestion on different routes to enable them to choose the best route for them to take to the coast.

The system required will be very much like that needed to control traffic lights in a town, except that the output will

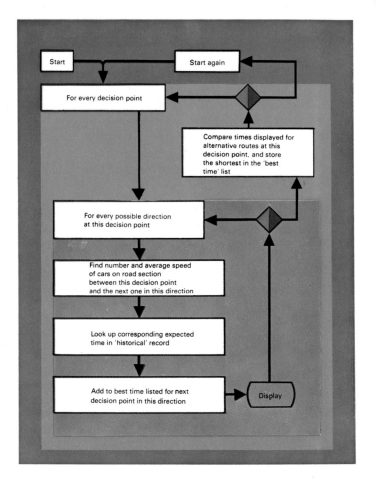

Flow chart for time display calculation

consist of advisory messages rather than mandatory commands. The detection system will be just the same as in the town situation, and it will be useful to have it set up in such a way that it gives speeds of vehicles as well as counting them. The systems for handling messages and passing them from one computer to the other will also be the same.

EXAMPLE OF BEST TIME CALCULATION

Suppose we have a road system like the one shown below, where the letters denote decision points and the numbers represent the expected times in minutes to traverse each road section

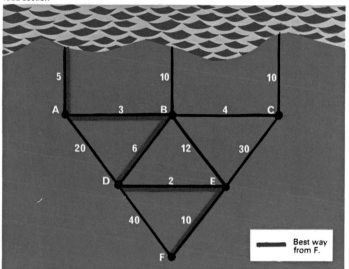

We will start working out times for the points nearest the sea:
for A, the possible times are 5 minutes (direct) and $3+10=13$
(via B), so the best time is 5 minutes. Similarly, for B we would
take $3+5=8$ minutes (via A) or 10 direct or $4+10=14$ (via C)
so the best time is 8 minutes; and so on for C, D, etc. The
resulting displays are shown below. Starting from F, the best
way would be via E, D, B and A, 26 minutes.

DISPLAYS AT EACH DECISION POINT

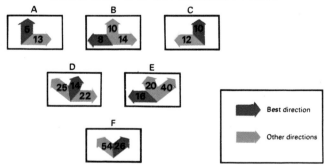

Switchgear

Generating sets

Boilers

Analog and
digital signals

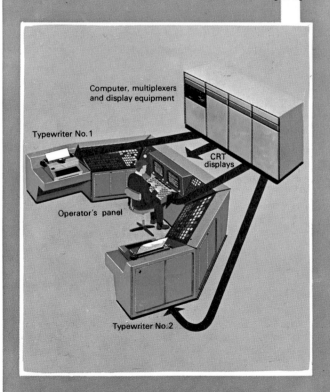

Computer, multiplexers
and display equipment

Typewriter No. 1

CRT
displays

Operator's panel

Typewriter No. 2

Layout of a computer system (*left*). Power station interior (*above*).

POWER STATIONS

Power stations, both conventional and nuclear-powered, have become increasingly complex in the last ten years. This complexity results from an ever-increasing demand for greater efficiency and for cheaper electricity. As a result, highly sophisticated instruments are now used in power station control rooms. And to control boilers, turbines and switchgear more effectively, large quantities of accurate information are required – information that can be scattered over a very large station. A large labour force would be required to note these readings and a computer can help here.

35

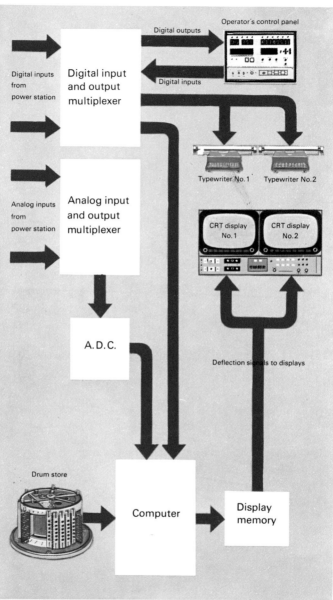

Operator's control panel

Digital outputs

Digital inputs

Digital inputs
from
power station

Digital input
and output
multiplexer

Typewriter No. 1   Typewriter No. 2

Analog inputs
from
power station

Analog input
and output
multiplexer

CRT display
No. 1

CRT display
No. 2

A.D.C.

Deflection signals to displays

Drum store

Computer

Display
memory

The type of computer needed is smaller and less comprehensive than those normally used in large scientific and business applications. These computers are made to be more rugged and have to withstand much greater extremes of temperature because they are in an industrial environment. One feature of such computers is an *interrupt system*, which enables the machine to respond in order of priority to demands for action from various external devices. The interrupt system can cause a program to jump to a special sub-program.

All the inputs from the power station are in either digital or analog form. An analog signal is one which uses a variable voltage or current to represent a variable signal. For example, one volt could represent a temperature of 100° centigrade; then half a volt will represent 50° centigrade. A digital signal is one that uses a number of on/off states to represent a binary number, proportional to the measurement being made.

The devices which convert measurements to analog or digital form are called *transducers*. Some single-event measurements may also be represented by digital inputs. For example, if a steam pressure rises too high, a safety valve is operated which causes a relay to close. If the relay is open it represents 'O', indicating a 'normal' condition, and if closed it represents '1', indicating an 'alarm' condition. In a typical system there may be thousands of inputs.

A device called a *multiplexer* selects the input required for feeding to the computer. Two multiplexers are needed, one for the digital inputs and one for the analog inputs. The multiplexer uses electronic switching circuits to feed into the computer only one input at a time at very high speeds.

If an analog signal is selected, some method must be used to convert the variable-voltage analog signal into a digital signal or word that can be recognized by the computer. Such a device is called an *analog-to-digital converter* (ADC). Some of the digital inputs may be used to control indirectly the total system in various modes of operation from an operator's panel mounted on the control room desk.

Example of an industrial power station data-processing system

The computer is linked directly to cathode-ray tube (CRT) displays which quickly present measurements to the operator. A CRT display rapidly writes characters on to a normal television-type tube. Computer words are transferred into a *buffer store* similar to the magnetic core store in the main computer. Part of the computer word represents the character to be written, and part the position of the character on the screen. The electronic logic of the display equipment scans around the buffer store, and writes the character found in each successive memory location at a speed of about 150,000 characters a second. The screen position, held in the buffer store with the characters, directs the beam before writing each character. The letter or figure to be written is formed by 'wobbling' the beam around a grid of squares. For example, the letter 'A' shown in the diagram is written by first switching the beam on, then moving it in fixed steps Sabcdefghjb, and then shutting off the beam for bjhg and on again for gkl.

Generation of characters on a cathode-ray tube (*below and opposite*)

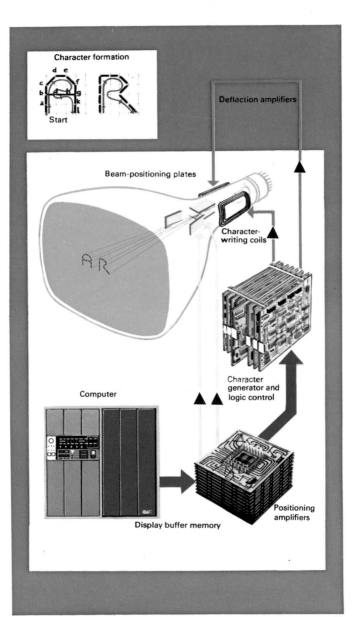

Character formation

d e
c   f
b   g
a   k
Start

Deflection amplifiers

Beam-positioning plates

Character-writing coils

Character generator and logic control

Computer

Positioning amplifiers

Display buffer memory

All the parts working together

All the equipment just described is controlled by a master program, called an *executive,* using the priority interrupt system. The executive acts like a central office, itemizing, sorting, filing, and giving instructions according to what has to be done. The main executive runs in the main core memory of the computer but may call on many smaller sub-programs which are stored on a magnetic drum. The magnetic drum is known as a bulk storage device, and works very much like a normal domestic tape recorder but very much faster. A typical magnetic drum can hold up to 500,000 computer words, whereas the memory inside the computer can hold only about 8,000 to 16,000 words.

One of the main tasks of the executive is to keep a calendar of real-time, so that the correct timing of the various functions can be carried out. A priority interrupt enables the executive to keep time from a signal generated every second by an electronic clock. The executive program normally runs in a loop, looking for functions to perform and waiting for interrupts. If no interrupts occur, no action is taken. In an average system, the loop takes as little as three-thousandths of a second to run through. Every second, an interrupt will occur from the real-time clock, causing the executive to take a *calendar program* from the drum store and place it in the computer memory. The calendar program keeps a permanent record of time in hours, minutes, and seconds, together with day, month, and year. Once the calendar program has been up-dated, the executive again takes over control of the equipment.

If the operator in the power station control room now requires a typeout of all the plant measurements at ten-minute intervals, he may dial this request to the computer from his panel. By dialling a certain code number and figures representing 'typeout interval' and 'ten minutes', an interrupt

A simplified diagram showing the operation of the executive. It continually runs in a loop. On receipt of an interrupt, the program exits into a sub-program, and then, if all tasks have been completed, goes back to the executive. Some programs may 'call' another program, which then calls yet another, and so on, until the task is completed.

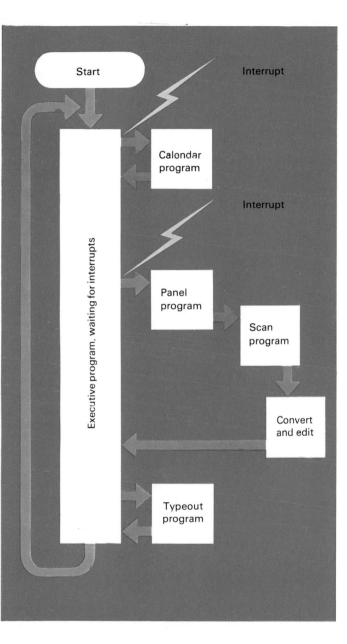

is given to the computer. As long as the computer is free from any other tasks of a higher priority, it selects the input from the panel and *reads-in* the information. This function is performed by yet another program called a *panel processing program* taken from the drum store. The program then examines the data just read-in to find out what course of action to take. In our example, the 'ten-minute' information is stored in a special location which is examined regularly when the calendar program is running to see if ten minutes have elapsed. If ten minutes are due, the executive is informed and a scan program is taken off the drum. Using this program, the required input points are scanned and the required data stored in a sequential group of memory locations known as a *table*. In this form, the data is said to be 'raw' as it has come directly from the plant. After the data has been scaled and corrected, a final program, the typeout routine, is used to type-out in numerical form all the plant measurements which were required.

In similar ways, the operator may ask the computer to put on to one of the CRT displays all the measurements concerned with, say, turbine speed. He would *dial-in* code numbers to request this new action, causing an interrupt as before. But this time, a different sub-program is taken from the drum store. This program takes all the information previously typed-out, and places it with the screen-position codes into the CRT display memory. The measurements now immediately appear on the screen.

The information concerning the turbine speed is brought up to date every few seconds, in case one of the measurements has changed while the operator has been looking at the original readings. This function is another job of the executive, which has remembered that a display is being given. Every few seconds the program will call up the scan program previously used, and eventually modify any characters in the display memory that have changed.

The range of functions of this sort of computer can be extended to include monitoring the station switchgear, performing daily calculations of operating efficiency, and checking to see whether any measurements have exceeded certain pre-arranged limits.

A further refinement can be added to such industrial computer systems to prevent the loss of vital information should the computer power supplies fail. Suppose the power supplies to the computer failed while a typewriter was operating. A special circuit 'sees' the voltage falling and warns the computer by the highest priority interrupt. Every fraction of a second that the computer power supplies fall below a certain level is significant as a computer can process an average of 500,000 instructions a second.

Having received the interrupt, the executive program now goes into a power failure routine. It stores all the conditions of its internal circuits, and then stops with plenty of time left before the power supplies finally reach a low level. When the computer starts again, the executive program picks up the threads of what it had been doing and continues to type-out what it was handling before the failure.

Power station control room

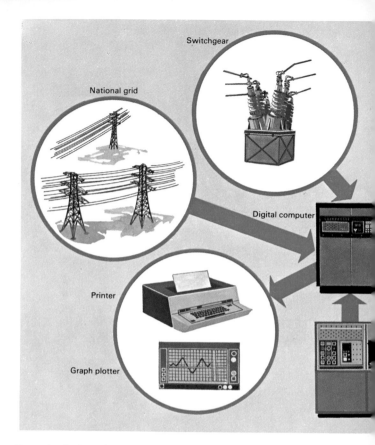

Example of what a future grid control system may look like

A computerized national grid

One future application of computers in the electrical supply industry is for systems to control the national electricity supply grid. Analog computers have been developed which simulate the country-wide supergrid of power lines, and if kept fed with up-to-date information can show the conditions to be expected in the grid network in the immediate future. If a generator or piece of switchgear fails, the information can be fed into the analog computer, plus future conditions (such as weather), to show the effects of future demand.

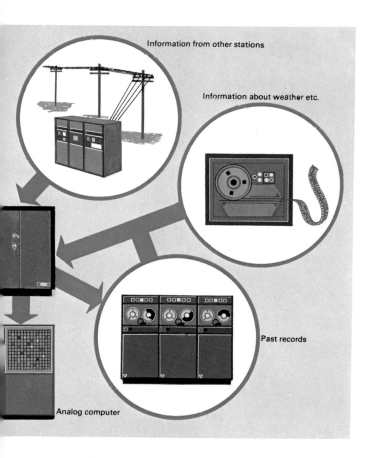

Information from other stations

Information about weather etc.

Past records

Analog computer

To feed information to the analog system, a digital computer in a *hybrid system* files and assesses all the input and output data. Signals come from the grid itself, switching gear, and other power stations. This information is assembled into meaningful signals to inject into the simulated grid system in the analog computer. Records of past conditions are stored on magnetic tape, and may be called upon for comparisons. The outputs of the analog computer are continuously processed by the digital computer to type-out trends.

PRINTING

The traditional methods of printing and editing involve a great deal of human effort – often to a strict time schedule, as in producing magazines and newspapers. Editors and writers compile a manuscript, which has to be retyped several times until the copy is finally approved in terms of content, style, and length. Big last-minute alterations mean that the whole document has to be retyped before submission to the printer.

Flow chart for typesetting by computer

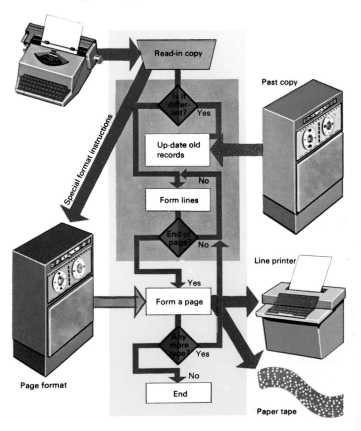

When a manuscript is finally set in print, the typesetter must take into consideration all the factors governing the layout of the type matter on the page. Generally the text is arranged in columns, so that the typesetter has to make sure that all the words on each line come within the width of the column. If a line is short, the typesetter 'pads out' the line by inserting larger spaces between the words. If the line is too long, he has either to put the 'overspill' word onto the next line or to 'break' a word on the end of a line by hyphenating it. Not all words can be broken however: for example one cannot split the word 'through' into two parts. The process of making all the lines of type exactly the same length is called *justification*. During justification, the typesetter has to avoid padding out each line in a similar way, causing 'rivers' of white paper to appear in vertical lines through the text.

If modifications to the text have to be made after typesetting, complete blocks of type have to be removed and the justification process carried out on the inserted text. All the existing type has to be 'moved on' and new end-of-column breaks and end-of-page breaks made.

Using a computer

A computer system can be applied to typesetting to perform the task of justification, and to keep a permanent record of the text so that modifications, additions and deletions can be made automatically. The system does not require a special computer, but uses special and sometimes involved programs. There are three main functions: generating lines of type, pages of type, and up-dating old files for modifications.

A typical layout of a flow chart for such a computer program is shown on page 46. A special typewriter is used which has, in addition to normal upper and lower case characters, special keys to assist in the page-forming process. The copy is typed into the computer, which assembles and stores all the characters. If the input is a modification to a previously processed piece of text, the past file will be up-dated and re-justified. If the input is new copy, the program starts to generate lines until the end of a page is reached. If any more copy is to be processed, the program returns to generating lines, until no copy is left to process.

As the words are typed into the computer, the characters and words are counted. When an end-of-word is detected by the arrival of a 'space' character, the program looks to see if enough characters have been read-in for that line. If not, more characters are accepted. When the end of a line is reached, one of two conditions has occurred: either the exact number of characters are on that line (no overflow), or the last word has made the line exceed the required number of characters. In the first case, the program sets up the next line and returns to the start. In the second, the computer compares the overflow word with a stored list of words that may be broken, and finds the correct place to hyphenate. If the word appears in this table, it is split and a hyphen added. The first part of the word with its hyphen is placed on the previous line, and the second part is used to start the next line. The original line-length may still need adjustment.

Constructing a line (*below*). Design of typical page format (*right*).

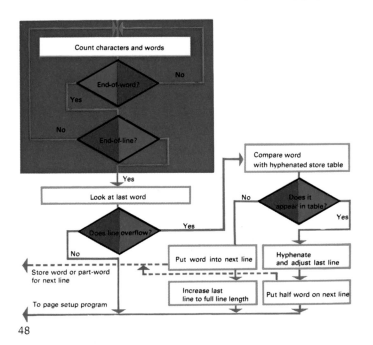

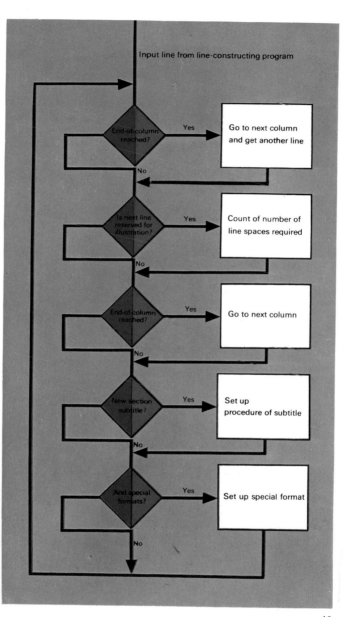

Input line from line-constructing program

End-of-column reached? — Yes → Go to next column and get another line

No

Is next line reserved for illustration? — Yes → Count of number of line spaces required

No

End-of-column reached? — Yes → Go to next column

No

New section subtitle? — Yes → Set up procedure of subtitle

No

And special formats? — Yes → Set up special format

No

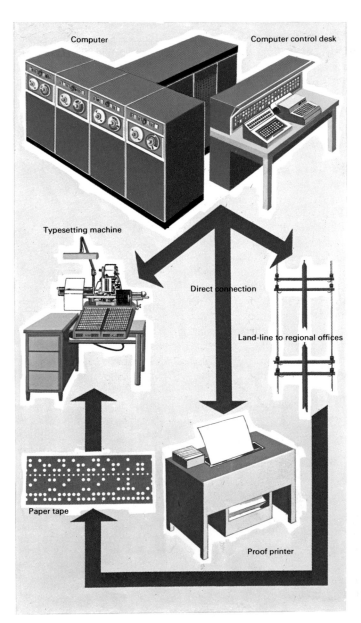

Computer

Computer control desk

Typesetting machine

Direct connection

Land-line to regional offices

Paper tape

Proof printer

If the word does not appear in the table of permitted word breaks, it cannot be hyphenated; it is placed at the beginning of the next line, and the former line is adjusted to the correct length by adding larger spaces between words. Spaces are varied between the words on following lines to prevent vertical bands of white ('rivers') from appearing in the text. Alternatively, the computer may print-out a request for instructions on how to break a word, and the information is stored for reference. Then the program begins the next line.

Setting up a page

As each line is formed, the page program looks to see if the end of a column of type has been reached. If it has, the next column is formed. But if this line number has been allocated for an illustration, a number of blank lines are inserted. This may result in a new column being required, and if so yet another column is set up. The program then looks to see if a heading or subheading is required. If so, spaces are inserted to separate the title from the rest of the text. Finally, any required special formats are taken into account. After completing this sequence, the computer forms another line, then again goes through the page-forming program.

The punched tape eventually generated by the computer contains all the instructions required to operate an automatic typesetting machine, or the computer may be connected directly to the typesetter. The punched tape or computer output serves exactly the same function as a keyboard-operated linotype machine. Alternatively, the computer output may be used to control a filmsetting machine which, instead of producing metallic type for letterpress printing, produces photographic negatives of a complete page of text. These are used to make plates for offset printing processes.

A central computer could control the typesetting or film-setting for several machines located in different places and linked to the central computer by telegraph lines. Or remote offices could transmit copy about local events directly to the central computer for setting in a national newspaper.

A typesetting/printing-by-computer system, showing how regional copy could be transmitted to the typesetter via a central computer

AIRLINES

This chapter begins with a description of the time-sharing remote access system used by airlines for making and recording seat reservations. It goes on to show how the same computer can deal with most of an airline's routine operations.

From the passenger's point of view, the existence of a reservation system means that he can enter an airline office or travel agency almost anywhere in the world, ask for a reservation, and get immediately either a confirmation of the reservation or information that the flight he required is fully booked.

From the travel agent's point of view, the remote enquiry system can save his staff a great deal of time, both in looking up information in complicated timetables and in communicating by telephone, telex, or mail with airlines about definite and provisional reservations and cancellations. At present, most enquiry systems deal only with the operations of one airline or group of airlines; but it seems likely that

A customer at a branch booking office asks for a reservation on a transatlantic flight. The clerk types the enquiry on the console keyboard, and gets an immediate display (*top right*) of the vacancies available and a ticket printed on the spot by a typewriter under remote control of the computer.

A clerk types a customer's travel enquiry on a keyboard—as she presses each key, the corresponding character is formed on the cathode-ray tube. She checks the message when complete before pressing the SEND key to transmit it to the computer.

```
DISPLAY ALL VACANCIES
LONDON · NEW YORK
TOURIST 21/6/68
```

The computer sends a reply immediately, which is displayed on screen until the clerk presses ERASE key. While the customer is thinking, one of the figures changes, showing that another booking has been made somewhere in the world.

```
LONDON - NEW YORK  21/6/68

FLIGHT   DEP   ARR   VACANCIES
                     1ST TRST
KB712   1035  1515    7    10
KK901   1350  1730    3     1
KB715   1500  2010    5    21
```

The clerk keys in the customer's order. The computer requests name and address and other details, which the clerk types and sends (note that the screen displays both the clerk's typed characters and the computer's replies and requests at the same time).

```
KK901  21/6/68
BOOK FIRM 1 TOURIST
NAME? MRS KATHLEEN JONES
ADDRESS? HYDE PARK HOTEL,
         LONDON
RETURN? OPEN
PAY BY? CASH
```

The computer confirms the booking and requests payment. When the clerk notifies payment, the computer prints a ticket on the hard-copy typewriter in the same branch office and informs the clerk by display that this has been done.

```
FLIGHT KK901 21/6/68
LONDON · NEW YORK 1 FIRM TRST
MRS KATHLEEN JONES
PLEASE PAY £115 · 15 · 0
PAID CASH
TICKET 34AV5986 PRINTED
```

The computer and communication centre at the international headquarters of the airline

Programming and data preparation

Independent travel agency

Confirmation by mail

Telephone enquiry

Aircraft fault necessitates

change of plan

Branch booking office

Telex message from maintenance

department

Aircraft fault necessitates

change of plan

Regional headquarters computing centre

Manager gets up-to-date
situation report on console

before long a travel agent will be able to have a computer console which can be connected to any of the major airlines' computer systems. When this system is operating, the airlines will have to accept that their competitors will always know the state of their reservation lists. It would seem that this possible commercial disadvantage will be a small one when set against the advantage of instant information, for passengers and travel agents, about flights with empty seats which might not be filled except through this interconnection of different computer systems.

From the airline's point of view, the existence of the remote enquiry system and of the central operational control system which goes with it means that the management can always know exactly details of reservations on all their flights. They can schedule additional relief flights for fully booked flights and inform the branch offices and agencies about this immediately. They can also minimize the cost of moving air crews and empty aircraft and the cost of accommodating them away from home. Many other operational economies can be provided once immediate information about all aspects of the system is available, and these can be monitored continuously by controllers and management.

Hardware

At an airline's headquarters, there will be a large computer complex with two or more processors using the same core store and disk store, as well as several message-switching computers. There will be magnetic tape units for archive storage in case of failure of the main storage system, and there will be a card input and printer and a graphical output for the central control and monitoring services.

At all the airline's offices and regional control centres there will be remote display consoles showing messages on television tubes, and *hard-copy* printers to give a permanent record of important messages. There will also be typewriter keyboards for the input of information and enquiries to the system. These will all be permanently connected by land-line or radio-link to the headquarters' computing complex.

Remote access system makes available late changes (*pages 54-55*).

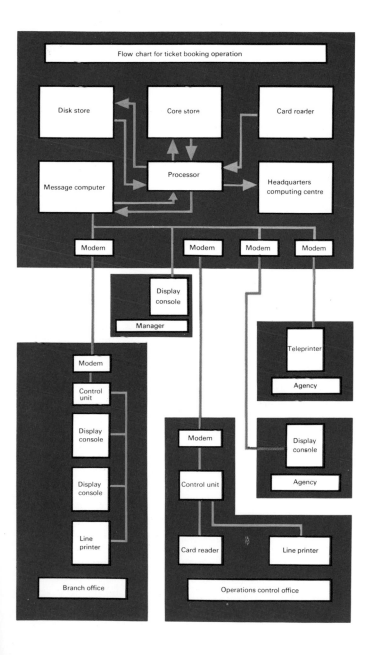

Flow chart for ticket booking operation

Disk store

Core store

Card reader

Message computer

Processor

Headquarters computing centre

Modem

Modem

Modem

Modem

Display console

Manager

Modem

Teleprinter

Agency

Control unit

Display console

Display console

Line printer

Branch office

Modem

Control unit

Display console

Agency

Card reader

Line printer

Operations control office

At the travel agency, there will be either a teleprinter or a remote console with a television-tube display and enquiry keyboard, but it need not be connected permanently to any particular airline's headquarters. It is possible to provide dialling equipment similar to that on a telephone, to enable the console to be connected to any of the major airlines' reservation systems. There may not be any hard-copy equipment at a travel agent's office, in which case confirmation copies of reservations and so on will be sent by mail from the airline's local branch office.

Regional headquarters of some international airlines may have their own computers, linked to the main headquarters system, to control local operations and to hold information about reservations for flights within the region. This would avoid overloading the international communication system and the central computer with regional transactions.

Equipment costs

For a major international airline, a whole system will cost millions of pounds and it will consist of the following.

(a) A multiprocessor time-sharing computer at the international headquarters, with duplicated message-switching computers. The multiprocessor computer will have a large main store, holding up to 2,000,000 characters, and a vast direct access disk-storage complex holding perhaps 1,000,000,000 characters of information. The value of the equipment at the international headquarters may well be over £2,000,000, although it would normally be rented from the computer manufacturers (for more than £500,000 per year) rather than be purchased outright.

(b) At up to about six regional headquarters, there would be smaller time-sharing computers and message-switching computers, costing about £500,000 for each region.

(c) At each branch office, there would be several display consoles and a hard-copy printer, with a total value of about £10,000.

(d) At a travel agency there would be a display console or teleprinter, costing £500 to £1,000.

(e) The communications equipment would be very costly, involving land-lines or radio-links, modems (modulator-demodulator units), and transmission control units. The communication cost would be a major part of the total cost to the airline, and might easily amount to £1,000,000 a year.

The great costs of the computing and communications system would nevertheless be more than offset by the huge savings resulting from being able to use aircraft, ground installations, and manpower with maximum effectiveness.

Core store
The programs and an index to the files will be kept in the core store, holding 1,000,000 to 2,000,000 characters, all accessible within a time of one microsecond or less. Any parts of the files to which reference is to be made must be copied from the disk store to the core store.

THE KEYPUNCH produces the coded representation of a character in one column when the corresponding key is pressed. This action also moves the punching head along to the next column. The key punch is 'off-line', that is. it is not connected to the computer.

THE CARD READER is connected to the computer. It senses the holes in the card by means of 'brushes' which press against it. A pattern of electrical pulses corresponding to the pattern of holes is sent to the computer. Often the card reader is built into the same machine as the card punch by means of which the computer can produce punched cards.

Disk store

The principal storage medium for the system is the magnetic disk pack. The most common type consists of six 14-inch disks mounted half an inch apart on a central hub and rotating at 2,400 revolutions a minute. Data is recorded on the disk surfaces (except the two outermost end surfaces) by means of magnetized spots in 200 concentric circular tracks on each surface. The pack can hold up to 25,000,000 characters and can transfer data to or from the processor at a rate of 156,000 characters a second once the read/write head is in the correct position. There are ten read/write heads, one for each surface, all mounted on one movable comb-like access mechanism which can move horizontally from the centre to the circumference. It takes an average of about one-tenth of a second for the head to get to the right position.

The disk pack is mounted on a drive unit, one type of which carries just one disk pack, while another type can

The disk pack is like a pile of gramophone records, but the information is stored magnetically. The comb-like read/write heads on the drive unit move horizontally, and read information from, or write information on to, the ten coated surfaces as the disks spin.

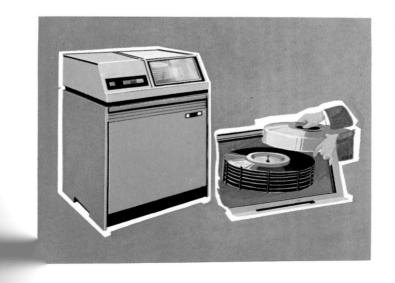

The display console has two main parts: the cathode-ray tube which shows letters and numbers formed by an electron-beam, and a typewriter-like keyboard. Characters are formed by the computer, as output, or by the operator using the keyboard, for input.

carry eight packs at once. The disk pack can be removed and replaced very simply for 'off-line' storage of information. This is a fairly expensive way of storing information, as each disk pack costs about £200 (which is about ten times the cost of magnetic tape to carry the same amount of information), but it is often worth doing because of the time saved when the disk pack is replaced for further processing.

There are also much bigger fixed disk units, which can contain more information, but they are not removable.

Display consoles

The most useful remote console for this application is not a typewriter but a display console, which gives a visible indication of the computer's responses on a cathode-ray tube. It is much quicker than a typewriter but does not give a permanent record of all messages; any hard-copy printout (tickets or invoices) must be made on a separate device.

Input of enquiries is done by a typewriter keyboard. An operator can compose and check messages on a screen before sending them to the computer.

The most common type of display console can show 200 to 1,000 characters, continuously generated by a control unit which can serve up to twenty consoles within 200 feet. Another type has a *storage scope*, which is slower but requires no regeneration and no separate control unit.

Input of data prepared 'off-line'

Although the computer files can be up-dated and interrogated from a remote console, most of the information contained in them and all the programs to handle them will be prepared as punched cards by 'off-line' equipment not connected to the computer. They can then be read-in by the card reader.

The computer is concerned with most aircraft ground activity.

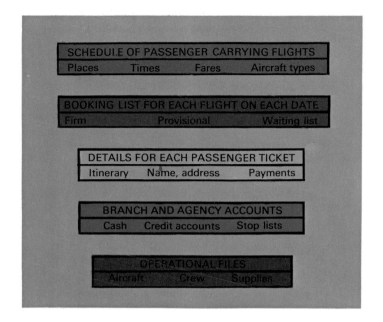

SCHEDULE OF PASSENGER CARRYING FLIGHTS			
Places	Times	Fares	Aircraft types

BOOKING LIST FOR EACH FLIGHT ON EACH DATE		
Firm	Provisional	Waiting list

DETAILS FOR EACH PASSENGER TICKET		
Itinerary	Name, address	Payments

BRANCH AND AGENCY ACCOUNTS		
Cash	Credit accounts	Stop lists

OPERATIONAL FILES		
Aircraft	Crew	Supplies

Files (A to E) stored in headquarters computer

Software

The main files in the central store are the following:-

(a) the flight schedule itself, indexed by airports of origin and destination (giving times of arrival and departure, type of aircraft, fare, and so on)

(b) for each flight on each day a separate list giving the booking position (indicating firm, provisional, and waiting-list bookings)

(c) separate records for each passenger ticket (giving itinerary, status of booking, payment details, and so on)

(d) the cash and credit accounts for branch offices, for travel agents, and for credit card agencies (with stop lists for bad debtors, stolen credit cards, and so on)

(e) operational files (giving details of aircraft movements, crew rosters, and supplies).

Files in a regional headquarters computer will be similar, but will refer only to operations in that region and international flights to and from that region.

Programs

There are two main types of programs required for the seat reservation system: those for initially setting up files in the store of the central computer, and those for handling enquiry and response and for up-dating the files with new reservations or cancellations. There are also programs for operational planning which use the same files, and which will be discussed later.

Flow charts

The flow chart on page 65 contains almost all the operations involved in the seat reservation system, and describes the whole story of a typical booking for a single flight not involving connections or break of journey.

Starting at the top right-hand corner, the top line deals with the establishment of files A and B. The middle box will be a very complicated program, which will take information about the airports to be connected and the frequency of flights to connect them, together with speeds, average weather conditions, congestion at airports, air-traffic rules, aircraft available, and so on. It will produce the detailed timetable for all the scheduled passenger-carrying flights.

The second line describes an enquiry about the timetable, such as 'What flights are there from Los Angeles to Sydney on Sundays?'. This type of enquiry, of course, could be handled by a printed timetable, but the availability of the computer enquiry system makes it possible for information about any changes in schedule to be very quickly available all over the world. The customer would consider the answer to this enquiry and then try to make a booking.

The next four lines of the flow chart describe the booking process. The request will specify the flight and date required, and the passenger's name and address which are used to establish a new record on file C for this passenger's ticket.

Flow chart for a typical single-flight transaction

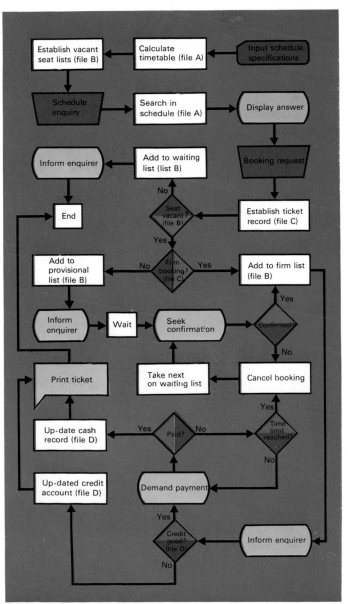

The computer will then examine the relevant record on file B to see whether or not there is a vacant seat on the required flight. If not, the passenger's reference number will be added to the waiting list for that flight on file B, a note will be made on his passenger ticket record on file C, and he will be informed via the agency console that he is on the waiting list.

If there is a seat vacant, the computer will examine file C to determine whether the booking is firm or provisional. If provisional, the passenger's reference number will be added to the provisional booking list in file B. The enquirer will be informed that he has a provisional booking and that he must confirm by a certain date. The process will then be suspended until either a confirmation is received or the closing date arrives, when a message will be sent to the console at the originating agency asking for confirmation. If no confirmation is received, the provisional booking will be cancelled and the next booking on the waiting list for the flight will be treated as a provisional booking while confirmation is sought.

The flow chart on page 67 again demonstrates the booking operation but this time it deals with a firm multi-flight booking using a credit card.

The flow chart on page 68 describes a more elastic enquiry, asking if there are any vacancies on a certain route on given dates. The program illustrated will either display all the vacancies on those dates, or, if there are none, find the flight with the shortest waiting list and display this information. Most of the subsections are the same as those on page 65.

Operational planning

At little extra cost, the computing system set up to deal with an airline's seat reservations can be made also to do a lot of the routine organizing of aircraft movements, crew rosters, supplies and other operational matters. Although most of these operations can be planned quite satisfactorily by ordinary manual methods, there are two particular advantages of the computer system: it can arrange to minimize the cost to the airline of carrying out the timetable (perhaps by trying out several ways of fulfilling the requirement

Flow chart for firm multi-flight booking using credit card

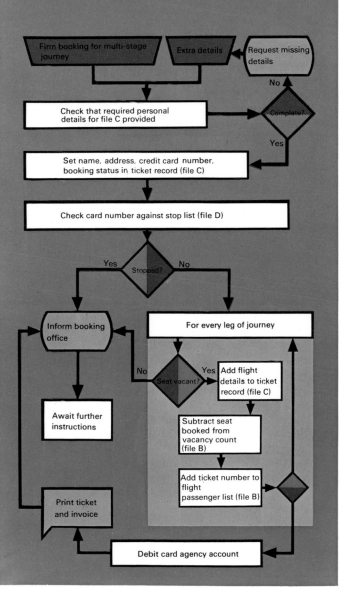

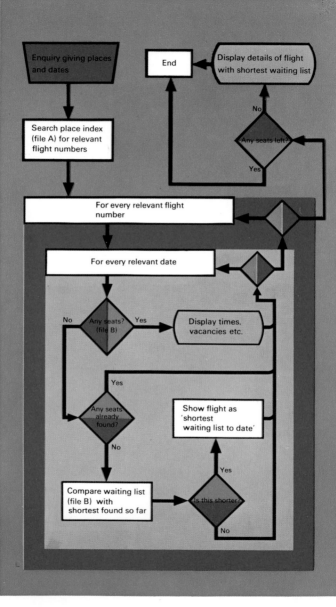

and comparing the costs of the different methods), and it can respond very quickly to changes in a situation caused, possibly, by the illness of a crew member or unscheduled maintenance on an aircraft. The computer will have available full information to produce a revised schedule for crew or aircraft very quickly, and the communication system connected to it can get the information on the changed movement orders to the relevant people with no delay.

Most of the operational functions of the computer will be performed by printing lists and rosters on the line printer, either at headquarters or at an operational control office, to be distributed to the people who will act on them. The main documents to be printed are described in the next section.

The passenger list will be used by the cabin crew and by the check-in counter staff at the airport of departure. It can be made completely up-to-date if required by sending console messages to the computer as the passengers check-in. As a

Flow chart for enquiry 'Any vacancies on a certain route on given dates ?' (*left*). Passenger list printed on the line printer (*below*).

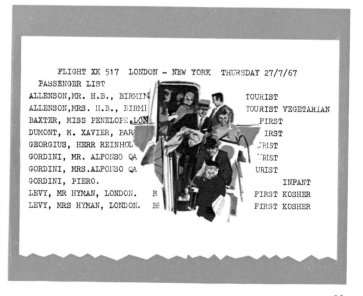

```
      FLIGHT XK 517  LONDON - NEW YORK  THURSDAY 27/7/67
      PASSENGER LIST
   ALLENSON,MR. H.B., BIRMIN                 TOURIST
   ALLENSON,MRS. H.B., BIRMI                 TOURIST VEGETARIAN
   BAXTER, MISS PENELOPE,LON                    FIRST
   DUMONT, M. XAVIER, PAR                       IRST
   GEORGIUS, HERR REINHOL                      URIST
   GORDINI, MR. ALFONSO QA                     URIST
   GORDINI, MRS.ALFONSO QA                    URIST
   GORDINI, PIERO.                                INFANT
   LEVY, MR HYMAN, LONDON.  B                 FIRST KOSHER
   LEVY, MRS HYMAN, LONDON.  BF               FIRST KOSHER
```

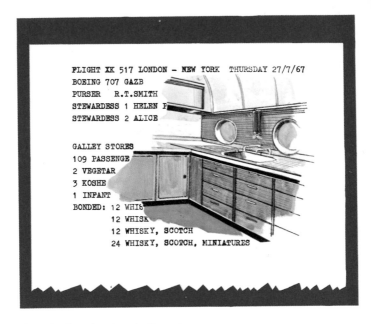

```
FLIGHT XK 517 LONDON - NEW YORK  THURSDAY 27/7/67
BOEING 707 GAZB
PURSER    R.T.SMITH
STEWARDESS 1 HELEN P
STEWARDESS 2 ALICE

GALLEY STORES
109 PASSENGE
2 VEGETAR
3 KOSHE
1 INFANT
BONDED: 12 WHI
        12 WHISK
        12 WHISKY, SCOTCH
        24 WHISKY, SCOTCH, MINIATURES
```

Supplies list printed on the line printer

result, any passengers who have not arrived at the airport do not appear on the list, and any passengers booking at the last minute can be included. As well as the name and journey details of each passenger, the list will indicate any special information for the cabin staff, such as the presence of infants, invalids, or anyone else requiring special care. An up-to-date passenger list is also essential in case accidents or other unforeseen events make it necessary to contact relations of passengers.

The supplies list would be used by all those loading or preparing the aircraft for its flight, including the catering staff, the storekeepers, the fuel attendants, and so on. The supplies needed would depend partly on the number of passengers and any particular requirements for diet, partly on the type of aircraft, and partly on the time and route of the flight. The amount of fuel required would depend on the time and distance and on the weather conditions, and the amount of freight would depend on the amount of fuel and the weight of the passengers and their luggage.

Aircraft movement orders will be produced some time in advance and will detail all the flights that the aircraft is due to make in the near future. They will also list all the regular maintenance and inspection requirements for the corresponding time, and will give suggestions as to what should be done. Of course, every inspection of the aircraft might indicate some faults to be repaired, and the computer will not be brought into this side of the operations at all. Information on jobs carried out will be passed to the computer, which will keep a serviceability record as part of the costing and equipment evaluation procedure of the airline. The aircraft movement order will also contain the names of the crew for each flight, and an up-dated version will be produced every time there is a change of crew roster. The computer can very quickly determine the availability of aircraft to replace

Aircraft movement orders printed on the line printer

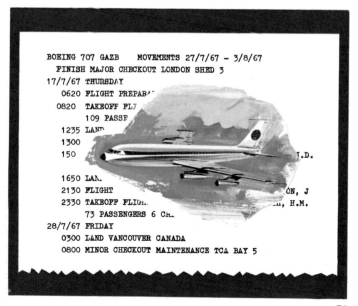

```
BOEING 707 GAZB    MOVEMENTS 27/7/67 - 3/8/67
   FINISH MAJOR CHECKOUT LONDON SHED 3
17/7/67  THURSDAY
   0620  FLIGHT PREPAR
   0820  TAKEOFF FLJ
         109 PASSE
   1235  LAN
   1300
   150                                           I.D.

   1650  LAN
   2130  FLIGHT                              ON, J
   2330  TAKEOFF FLIG                        H.M.
         73 PASSENGERS 6 CH
28/7/67  FRIDAY
   0300  LAND VANCOUVER CANADA
   0800  MINOR CHECKOUT MAINTENANCE TCA BAY 5
```

FLIGHT XK 517 LONDON - NEW YORK THURSDAY 27/7/67
BOEING 707 GAZB

CAPTAIN   MINELLI, RALPH J.
COPILOT   PARKES, MICHAEL
NAVIGATOR   JONES, CLIVE
RADIO   ANSTEY, JOE
PURSER   SMITH, ROBERT
STEWARDESS QUANTON, HELEN P.
STEWARDESS ROBERTS, ALICE

INDIVIDUAL MOVEMENT ORDERS

DUTIES 27/7/67 - 3/8/67
CAPTAIN RALPH J MINELLI
    THURSDAY 27/7/67 CAPTAIN BOEING 7
        0700 LONDON OCEANIC
        0820 TAKEOFF FLIGHT XK 517 NE   07
        1235 LAND KENNEDY NEW YORK
    FRIDAY 28/7/6'   DUTIES 27/7/67 - 3/8/67
        REST   CAPTAIN MICHAEL PARKES
                          THURSDAY 27/7/67 COPILOT BO

            -3/8/67
            C JONES
        '7/67 NAVIGATOR BOEING 707
        LONDON OCEANIC
        TAKEO
    35 LAND   DUTIES 27/7/67 - 3/8/67
        /7   STEWARDESS HELEN P QUANTON
        KEN   THURSDAY 27/7/67 FIRST S
        TAK   0720 LONDON OCEANIC
                           0820 TAKEOFF FLIGHT
                        'D KENNEDY NEW
                                SECOND
DUTIES 27/7/67 - 3/8/67   Y
PURSER ROBERT SMITH   65 RIO DE JANIERO
    THURSDAY 27/7/67 PURSE
        0720 LONDON OCEANIC
        0820 TAKEOFF FLIGHT
        1235 LAND KENNEDY NEW

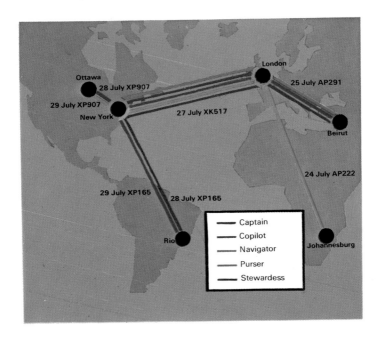

Individual orders (*left*) organize crew before and after Flight XK517.

any unexpectedly taken out of service, even if the replacements are at bases some distance away.

The crew rosters will be produced in two forms: a list of the whole crew for a specific flight, and individual notifications to each crew member about his whole programme for the next few weeks. The computer will have to take into account the regulations about the number of hours to be flown by pilots and air crew as well as the requirements of the airline's flight timetable. There will also be holidays, training periods, resignations, and other foreseeable events affecting the availability of crews which the computer can take into account in the forward planning. Unforeseeable events, such as illness and accident, can be allowed for very quickly by the computer, perhaps enabling the airline to reduce the number of stand-by crews. Sometimes it is necessary for crew members to take a 'wasted' journey in paid time to get to the

EXAMPLE OF OPTIMIZATION OF AIRCRAFT MOVEMENT

We want to allocate aircraft to maintain the given schedule.
There are several possible ways of organizing this, using different
numbers of aircraft. Three possible ways are shown below: clearly
the third is the most economical use of aircraft if these are the only
flights required. We are assuming in each case that the type of
aircraft is the same and that it takes one hour to prepare an aircraft
for take-off when it has just landed.

REQUIRED SCHEDULE

dep	0900		London	● ↑	arr		1800 ↑	
arr	1100		↓Amsterdam	●	dep		1600	
dep	0800		London	● ↑	arr		1700 ↑	
arr	1000		↓Brussels	●	dep		1500	
dep	1200	1300	Amsterdam	● ↑	arr	1200	1500 ↑	
arr	1300	1400 ↓	Brussels	●	dep	1100	1400	

| MOVEMENTS | 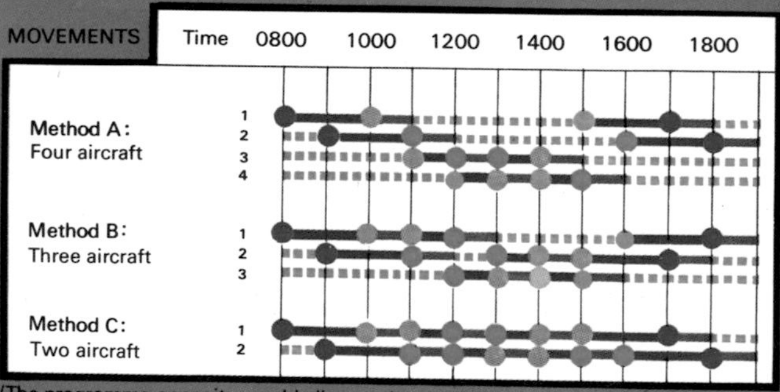 Time | 0800 | 1000 | 1200 | 1400 | 1600 | 1800 |

Method A:
Four aircraft — 1 2 3 4

Method B:
Three aircraft — 1 2 3

Method C:
Two aircraft — 1 2

(The programme opposite would allocate the aircraft by method C)

Key: ▬▬ in flight   ▬▬ ground preparation   ▪▪▪▪ wasted

Flow chart for optimization of aircraft movement (*right*)

place where their duty commences. The computer should be
able to minimize the number of occasions on which this
occurs by juggling the roster so that every duty begins at the
last location of the crew member concerned.

Given the flight timetable, the computer can calculate the
most economical way of fulfilling it with the aircraft available.
It should have done this, of course, in making up the timetable in the first place as well as in producing the aircraft

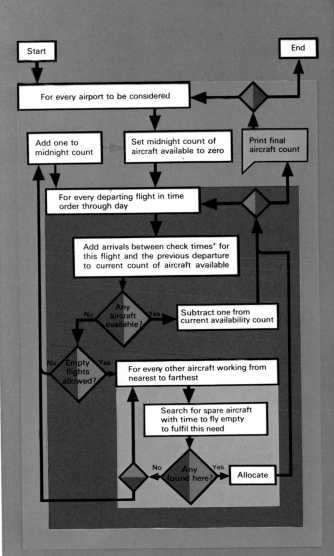

Start

End

For every airport to be considered

Add one to midnight count

Set midnight count of aircraft available to zero

Print final aircraft count

For every departing flight in time order through day

Add arrivals between check times* for this flight and the previous departure to current count of aircraft available

Any aircraft available?

No — Yes

Subtract one from current availability count

Empty flights allowed?

No — Yes

For every other aircraft working from nearest to farthest

Search for spare aircraft with time to fly empty to fulfil this need

Any found here?

No — Yes

Allocate

*'Check time' is taken as one hour before departure—it is the time allowed for aircraft turn round procedures.

movement orders. The program described on pages 74 and 75 is assumed to be doing this, but a very similar flow chart would be included in the original timetabling program. The example given assumes that every flight requires the same type of aircraft, and that the minimum turnround time is one hour. We may allow spare aircraft to fly empty from any airport with a surplus to another with a shortage.

Reaction to emergency

There will be two main types of action to be taken by the computing system in the event of an emergency – either a major one caused by a crash or a minor one caused by an aircraft found to be unserviceable just before loading. The first type of action will be to revise the operational orders for the airline's own equipment and personnel; the second type will be to try to transfer passengers or urgent freight to other airlines, or to charter additional aircraft.

For the first type of action, the operations controller will inform the computer through a console of the flight affected and the nature of the incident, and will request any additional aircraft or crew needed. The computer will examine the files and determine whether the request can be met without affecting other flights. If this is not possible, it will inform the controller and ask for his directions about priorities – whether it is more important for the interrupted flight to continue immediately or for all the other flights to continue as scheduled. If he directs the computer to produce a new operations schedule which changes other flights, it will try various permutations and choose the one which causes disruption to the smallest number of passengers.

The second type of action will be much easier if different airlines' seat-reservation computers are interconnected. If this is the case, the first airline's computer can request information on the booking position of any relevant flights on other airlines through their computers, and immediately make and confirm the required bookings. The information on whether this is feasible can be provided for the controller very quickly.

Computer's part in airline's reaction to emergency

Airliner crashes

Notification
and progress
reports

Operations controller

1. enquiry about spare
   resources

2. orders for
   re-allocation

Information
about changed
bookings

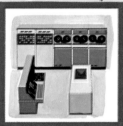

Stranded passengers
at later airport on
crash route

Headquarters computer
schedules planes as
requested by controller,
prints passenger list
for relative notification
and requests bookings
on another airline for
stranded passengers.

Revised
heading
information

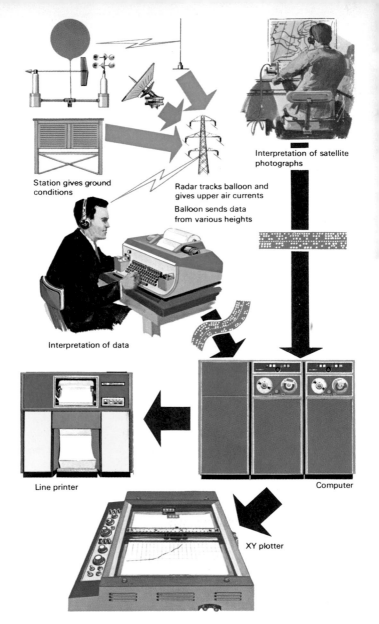

Interpretation of satellite photographs

Station gives ground conditions

Radar tracks balloon and gives upper air currents

Balloon sends data from various heights

Interpretation of data

Line printer

Computer

XY plotter

78

Chart preparation by computer (*left*). A balloon goes up from a weather ship in the North Atlantic (*above*).

WEATHER FORECASTS

For many years, weather forecasting used to be considered more of an art than a specific science. The age of the computer and the satellite has made forecasting much more accurate and has enabled us to make long-term weather predictions.

Short-term forecasts

Predicting weather basically involves making a three-dimensional map of all the conditions in a large volume of atmosphere at a certain point in time. By analysing the movements of air masses and disturbances from a series of such maps, a meteorologist can predict the future shapes of the map. To construct these maps, observations are made using weather ships and stations, equipped with ground measuring equipment, balloons, rockets, and radar, all taking measurements every three, six, or twelve hours. Temperature, pressure, visibility, wind speed and direction, humidity, and cloud cover are all recorded and transmitted to a central receiving station.

At the receiving station, all the incoming data is typed onto punched tape and fed into a computer, which analyses the data and selects all the points with the same barometer (pressure) readings to form a chart of surface pressure.

Alternatively, a device called an *XY plotter* may be used to draw lines of constant pressure on a map. An XY plotter is normally used to draw graphs; a pen mounted on a carriage can move vertically and horizontally over a flat surface upon which a sheet of graph paper is positioned. Computer instructions move the pen left or right and up or down by a few thousandths of an inch at a time, hence the alternative name of *incremental plotter*.

Charts are traced for various altitudes, so that a complete three-dimensional map of conditions is available for every three hours. A trained meteorologist can now use this rapidly prepared data to predict future air movements and precipitation conditions such as fog, snow, and rain. Over the large land and sea areas that are covered by such a system, no account can be made of local conditions. But the trained observer, freed from the task of having to prepare the charts himself, now has much more time to interpret his data and superimpose local variations.

Predicting long-term trends

For predictions up to thirty-six hours into the future, the system just described can be fairly accurate. This is because once a pattern, such as an anticyclone, has formed, the meteorologist can follow the pattern and predict how it might change for periods of up to thirty-six hours. After this time, the predictions become less reliable.

One possible method of predicting long-term weather conditions is to use old records and look for similar trends to those prevailing at the moment. A computer can speed up such a record search by sequentially eliminating data from its files.

The present weather conditions, taken from a series of charts for perhaps a week, are fed into a computer as punched

Flow chart showing method of selecting past records which resemble present weather conditions

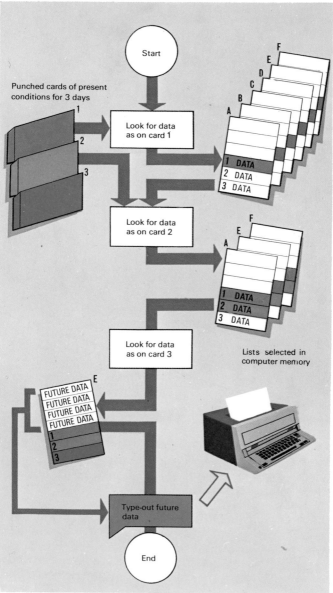

Start

Punched cards of present conditions for 3 days

1

2

3

Look for data as on card 1

F
E
D
C
B
A

1 DATA
2 DATA
3 DATA

Look for data as on card 2

F
E
A

1 DATA
2 DATA
3 DATA

Look for data as on card 3

Lists selected in computer memory

E
FUTURE DATA
FUTURE DATA
FUTURE DATA
FUTURE DATA

1
2
3

Type-out future data

End

8

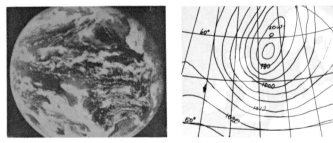

A weather satellite (*top*), a satellite-transmitted picture of cloud patterns (*left*) and a weather-map drawn with this information (*right*).

cards. For the sake of illustration, imagine that only three are used, representing conditions for the last three days and numbered one, two, and three. The computer takes the data from card one and searches its files for a similar set of data.

It may come up with six similar conditions A to F, and each of these sets of data will have an associated 'list' of conditions for the days or even months preceding it. The second day's data is then taken and the computer searches the second-day data of each of the lists A to F to find a similar condition. Perhaps A, E, and F were similar. The computer then takes data for day three and again looks for similar data on day three of the remaining 'lists'. Only one may now remain, let us say E. The computer examines this list to see which conditions prevailed for the days following day three and prints-out this data for examination as the basis of a long-term forecast.

Rainfall prediction

To predict rainfall is no easy task, as a great many complicated mathematical calculations are involved. The basis for these calculations is taken from measurements made at points on an imaginary fine grid network drawn over the country. Measurements of rainfall are made at points on this grid (thirty miles apart) and all this data, together with other meteorological data, is fed into a computer. At the present time, the computing power required to solve completely the complex problems involved is enormous; even with very powerful systems, about ten hours of computing time are required to make a daily rainfall forecast. But in years to come, as computer power increases, rainfall forecasts may be computed in only half an hour, making this technique a practical proposition.

World-wide satellite system

In spite of all the work on weather forecasts being done by computers today, a great deal more data is required to enable accurate forecasts to be made and this can only be achieved by collecting meteorological data on a world-wide scale. Today, only a fifth of the earth's surface has a reliable weather data collection service. To know more about how air masses move, data from all over the surface is required, and not just local data. The introduction of weather satellites has increased the amount of available information, so that cloud formations and hence air movements can be now observed directly. But satellites move in fixed paths, and although three are now in use, a rapidly-forming weather pattern may be missed. Also satellites can only observe and cannot make direct measurements. But when a world-wide satellite system has been achieved, really reliable weekly weather forecasts will begin to be more than wishful thinking.

MEDICAL AUTOMATION

The medical profession offers many opportunities for computers to increase the efficiency and effectiveness of hospital care. There are two types of application: nursing supervision, and complete data processing.

Hospital paper-work 'on-line'

Many hospital staff have the time-consuming job of maintaining up-to-date records of medical and administrative data. A great deal of information is generated by various hospital departments for any one patient and records are kept from the moment a patient is admitted. A general practitioner's letter may be the first piece of data to be collected, followed by an admission form and any other relevant ex-hospital information. This paper-work is filed and later added to with doctors' notes and possibly clinical data, such as results of X-ray examinations, blood tests, and heart waveform records.

To put all this information 'on-line' to a system involves using a powerful computer with large storage facilities and flexible data communications, because a lot of remote equipment has to have access to the computer. One type of data communications terminal is the keyboard CRT display. This type of information-enquiry station consists of a type-writer keyboard, used to type characters directly into the computer along a normal telephone cable, and a display.

A master program controls all the various input, filing, calculating, and output functions of the system. When a patient is admitted, his notes are simply 'keyed-in' to the system by typing a code number for that patient and entering the data. As more data is generated, the departments concerned simply type-in information about the patient as and when it becomes available. Eventually a mass of data is assembled for each patient, and is indexed by the computer.

Research workers can use the system for mathematical and record-searching work by using a time-sharing feature of such large systems. Some large computers are called *multiprocessors* and are really several computers in one. One of the

A hospital data collection system can assemble and index the mass of medical and administrative data generated by various departments.

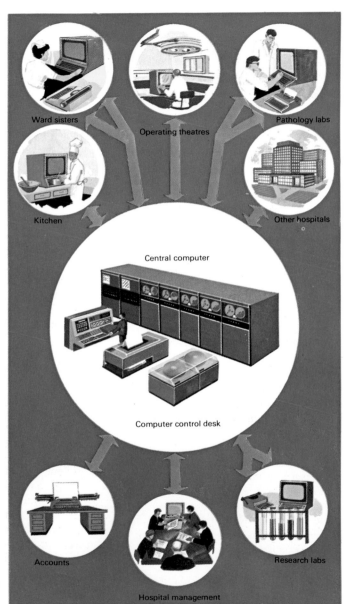

Ward sisters

Operating theatres

Pathology labs

Kitchen

Other hospitals

Central computer

Computer control desk

Accounts

Hospital management

Research labs

processors or small computers can perform one computation while the rest are performing other tasks. One of the processors is reserved to control the functions of all the rest. Different programs for separate jobs are manipulated in the multiprocessor memories in such a way that each operator uses the computer as if the program needed for his job were the only one being run in the memory.

Administrative offices would have access to the system to keep records and compute future bed and theatre allocations. By simply keying-in a request, data would be displayed from lists in the system store showing when and where a bed and theatre time would be available. The lists would be automatically up-dated every time a new booking was entered.

The system can perform the drug-checking procedures normally carried out on paper and prevent incorrect dosages by not releasing any information until a request or check has been made from two enquiry stations, one of which is under the control of a person in authority.

To prevent an unauthorized person from using an enquiry station, each station has a plastic-card reader, similar to a factory clocking-in machine. A person nominated to use the system has a card punched with a personal code which is recognized by the computer before access is given.

Patients 'on-line'

Modern surgery has increased the need to have more measurements made of a patient's condition during and after a large operation. At present, intensive-care units employ several qualified people for each patient to measure and record blood pressure, temperature, respiration and pulse rate. A small computer can provide what is known as a *supervisory system* to 'watch' all these body functions, raising an alarm if any measurement strays beyond certain limits. The important measurements generally taken are blood pressure, pulse rate, heart waveform from an electrocardiograph (ECG), respiration rate and volume of air breathed, and electroencephalograph (EEG) signals.

Intensive-care system: respirator (A), volume of air breathed (B), EEG (C), blood pressure (D), respiration (E), pulse rate (F), ECG (G).

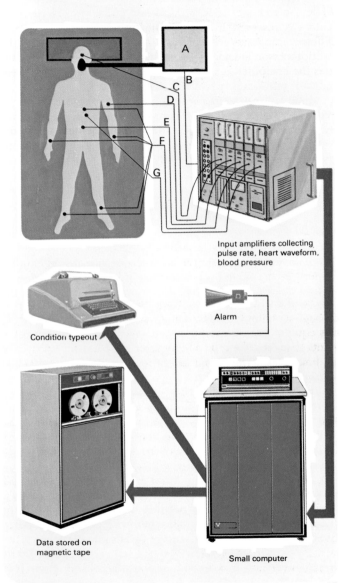

Input amplifiers collecting
pulse rate, heart waveform,
blood pressure

Condition typeout

Alarm

Data stored on
magnetic tape

Small computer

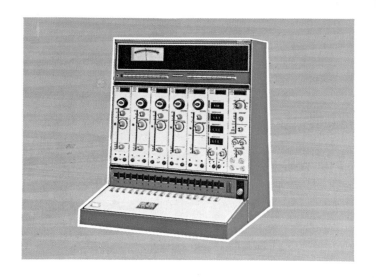

Console for supervising system controlling bodily functions (*above*).
Waveform analysis (*right*).

Measurements are taken from the patient and amplified through a computer input switch called a *multiplexer*. Using this equipment, the computer can select any measurement it wants to make. The type of computer used has a memory size of about 12,000 words and can process an average of 700,000 instructions in one second.

Often in this type of application the *shapes* of the various waveforms entering the computer are of great importance. The ECG waveforms provide information about how the patient's heart is working. It is therefore necessary for the computer to be able to detect changes in shape of the waveforms and not just to measure voltage levels.

A typical heart waveform cycle lasts for 0·8 seconds and by sampling this waveform every forty-four milliseconds, a reasonable likeness to the original shape may be made in digital form. The sampling process in the input to the computer involves changing the input voltage signals into digital form for each input channel. Modern systems can carry out 50,000 of these conversions in a second, so that the sampling rate just

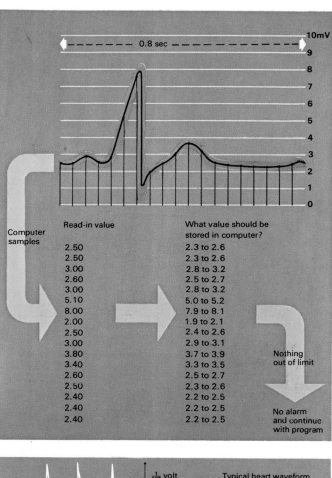

Computer samples	Read-in value	What value should be stored in computer?	
	2.50	2.3 to 2.6	
	2.50	2.3 to 2.6	
	3.00	2.8 to 3.2	
	2.60	2.5 to 2.7	
	3.00	2.8 to 3.2	
	5.10	5.0 to 5.2	
	8.00	7.9 to 8.1	
	2.00	1.9 to 2.1	
	2.50	2.4 to 2.6	
	3.00	2.9 to 3.1	
	3.80	3.7 to 3.9	Nothing out of limit
	3.40	3.3 to 3.5	
	2.60	2.5 to 2.7	
	2.50	2.3 to 2.6	
	2.40	2.2 to 2.5	No alarm and continue with program
	2.40	2.2 to 2.5	
	2.40	2.2 to 2.5	

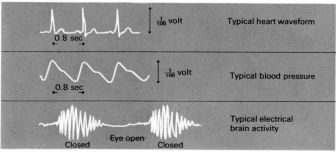

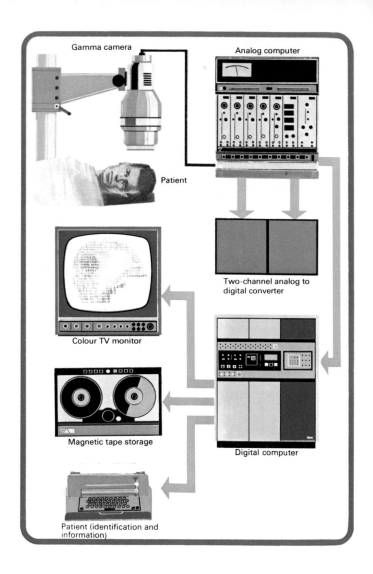

Gamma camera

Analog computer

Patient

Two-channel analog to
digital converter

Colour TV monitor

Digital computer

Magnetic tape storage

Patient (identification and
information)

Slightly more powerful radioactive signals emitted from a malignant
growth are located by a gamma camera, analysed by an analog
computer and converted to digital signals for display and storage.

quoted is very slow in comparison. This means that the
computer can handle 700,000 × 0·044, that is, 30,800
instructions between each sample. Even if it is doing a
similar analysis on five other channels, it can still perform
30,800 ÷ 5, that is, 6,160 instructions between each sample
on each channel. This gives ample time to examine the entering waveform. Each time an input sample is made, a small
compare program is used to see if the measured value lies
within certain limits, representative of a correct waveform.
If any input waveform is distorted, a remote audio alarm
sounds and a typeout of the condition is made.

Locating tumours by computer
The combination of two branches of technology, computer
science and atomic physics, has resulted in a powerful and
rapid method of finding tumours at an early stage and when
treatment can be most effective. Some radioactive isotopes

Enlargement of television monitor showing tumour to rear of brain

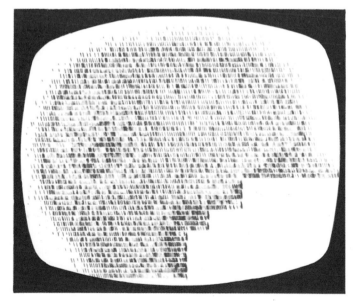

tend to gather in malignant tumours, so that after introducing such substances into the body, the tumour will become slightly more radioactive than the surrounding organs and tissues. A *gamma camera* is used to pinpoint the location of this radioactivity. The camera has a number of detectors sensitive to the particular radiation being emitted and is supported above the patient. The detectors directly above the tumour will receive more radiation than those in other areas. An analog computer analyses all these signals, and eventually produces two other signals representing one cell on a sixty by sixty grid of cells over the patient. As the measurement continues, more signals will arrive into the cells corresponding to the area of the tumour than into those of other areas.

Diagnosis by computer

Diagnosis is a controversial subject to which the medical computer can be applied. The computer could never replace a doctor, who meets a patient face to face and can gain much diagnostic information by simply seeing and talking to him. The intention would be to give doctors yet another diagnostic tool – to assist rather than replace.

No human being can remember everything, and most of us quickly forget what we learn when not using that information. Doctors must therefore spend time referring to text books and collecting information. A computer can store and provide indexing for a large medical library. Taken a step further, the computer can even provide a general diagnostic routine for the doctor to follow.

Unfortunately, diagnostic decisions made by a computer can only be based on yes/no answers and questions. In practice, various factors may cloud such straightforward decisions; some symptoms may not appear, others may mislead. The computer must not therefore make the absolute decision, but aid the doctor to decide more quickly.

Flow chart of how a diagnostic program might work. The actual route followed would depend on the symptoms. The doctor would still be in absolute charge and might choose to ignore computer results because he had overriding information.

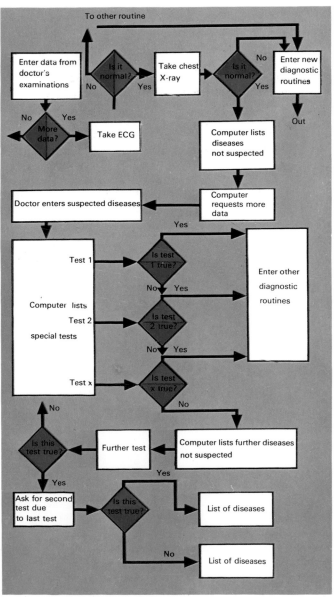

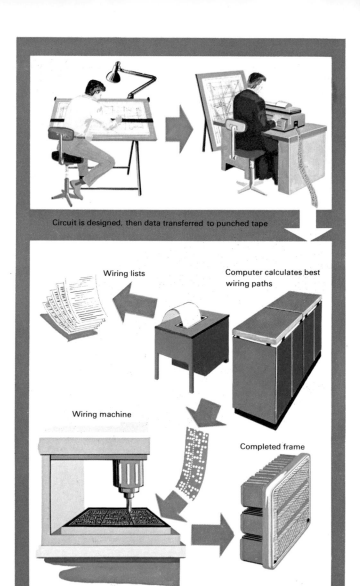

Circuit is designed, then data transferred to punched tape

Wiring lists

Computer calculates best wiring paths

Wiring machine

Completed frame

COMPUTERS FOR MAKING COMPUTERS

The idea of computers making themselves may sound like science fiction, but computer manufacturers are finding that the computer itself can take over a lot of repetitive and uninteresting tasks from the human operators. And the control of the operation still lies with human engineers.

Automatic wiring

The heart of a computer is the *central processor*, and this is the part that performs all the logic, memory control, and arithmetical calculations. The logic circuits for the central processor are mounted on printed-circuit boards, which plug into an array of sockets on the *main-frame*. In a small computer this frame has space for about 200 boards and larger systems have many more. It also has the necessary wiring connections, about 5,000 in all, made with wrapped joints. A wrapped joint is made by wiring a single strand of wire round a square pin with sharp corners. As the wire bends at the

Automatic wiring system for producing computer logic files (*left*).
A complicated circuit which has been automatically wired (*below*).

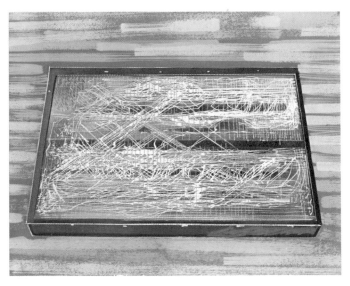

A computer-controlled automatic wiring machine

corners, it exerts a high pressure on the sharp edge and makes a tiny weld.

Each main-frame for every computer is generally wired with all the connections the same. Making these wired frames is therefore a repetitive job. A computer-produced program may be used to do the wiring in a fraction of the time taken by wiremen. Making such a system starts with the logic designer, who prepares the original logic drawings for the computer. A punched-tape operator then uses these drawings to put details of the interconnections onto punched tape, which is then analysed by computer. The computer performs three functions: it works out the shortest and most economical way of making the interconnections, it types-out a list of these interconnections for checking purposes, and it generates a punched tape of instructions to the wiring machine. The tape program is fed to the machine, which makes all the wiring connections automatically, in sequence.

Automatic memory checking

Computer memories are normally made of small ferromagnetic beads or *cores* threaded into a matrix network. When sufficient current is fed through a selected core, it becomes magnetized and stays magnetized. In this way, it stores a 'bit' of data, say the digit '1'. If a current is driven in the opposite direction through the core, it becomes demagnetized and sends a small current along a *sense-wire* threaded through the core; this represents the contents of that memory location.

There may be hundreds of thousands of cores in the smallest memories, and one problem for the computer designer is to find the optimum currents to switch all the cores on and off. Even if all the cores are made at the same time in the same manufacturing conditions and from the same materials, they vary slightly in the current needed to turn them on and off. Taking into account the best and worst possible conditions,

Memory elements for computers can be checked using other computers.

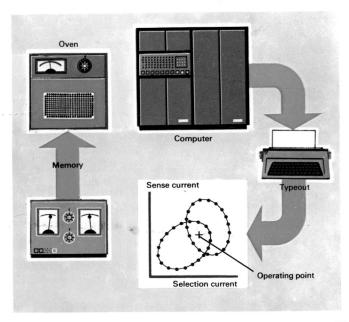

we can find an area of operation in which the operating currents must lie. One of the difficulties is that this area varies with temperature. A graph which shows the area is nicknamed a 'Schmoo-chart'.

By using a computer, the selection currents can be individually varied in a test memory until the memory fails. The failure indicates that one core has not turned on or off, and the boundary of the operation area has been found. The variation of currents is continued until enough points have been collected to plot the Schmoo-chart at a given temperature. The whole operation is repeated at another temperature to obtain a second chart. The two graphs may then be compared to find the best current settings for that particular memory.

Automatic board checking

It was stated previously that all the logic circuits in a computer are mounted on printed-circuit boards of various types. A working computer may also be used to check the correct functioning of these circuits as they are manufactured.

Most of the boards perform what are called *logic functions* – that is, an output voltage is generated by a certain set of input conditions and only by those conditions. The logic function of a board is checked by a test computer which switches the required voltages onto the inputs of the board. If the output voltage generated is incorrect, the computer prints-out a 'reject' message.

In practice, logic boards may have several logic functions and various combinations of input and output signals have to be checked. Rejected boards are examined to find the faulty component, which is then replaced; the board is re-checked and passed if satisfactory.

Computers checking themselves

One common technique for checking completed computers is to use a *diagnostic program,* which is run in the machine being checked to reveal any faults.

A *memory diagnostic* is a program which tests every memory location in the computer with every number that can possibly be stored. First of all, the program loads every location with '1', then reads back all these locations to see if they still

A micro-circuit — shown here about ten times actual size

contain the original number. Then '2' is stored in every location and the sequence repeated, and so on. If a bad location is detected, a typeout is made showing where the fault has occurred. This diagnostic program is usually run at various temperatures, to show whether or not the computer is working in the correct area of the Schmoo-chart.

An *instruction-check program* detects computer instructions that are not working correctly. This program sequentially tests each instruction to see if it is performing all the required logic functions in the computer. For instance, an 'add' instruction is performed on various known numbers and the answer compared with the expected answer. If the answer is correct, the program goes on to the next instruction, perhaps a 'multiply'. If an instruction is not interpreted correctly, the program types-out details of the failure. These types of diagnostic program have a limited use. For example, a memory test program needs part of the memory to store the program, as does the instruction-check program.

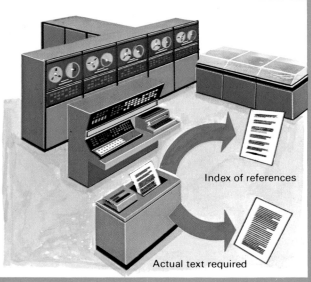

Index of references

Actual text required

INFORMATION RETRIEVAL

As modern society progresses, more and more information is generated in all fields of technology, administration, and the professions. Many thousands of scientific papers and text books are published every year in many languages on every possible technical subject. Businesses, the law, and government departments generate even more printed matter than do the sciences. All this information has to be stored in files and libraries.

To obtain some particular data from all this mass of information is now becoming a major task for both the searcher and the librarian. In this chapter, we shall examine some of the ways in which a computer can store and index information in order to make the quick retrieval of relevant material possible.

A legal library

Of all the sources of information mentioned previously, the legal profession generates the greatest amount of data. Members of this profession often have to sort through masses of information concerning statutes, previous legal decisions, and statements and discussions of legal topics. One difficulty is to sort out not only the relevant subjects but also those that *might* contain relevant information. To aid in searching legal texts, libraries use complicated indexing systems.

There are two possible ways in which legal information retrieval may be achieved using a computer. The indexing system can be stored on magnetic tape and a computer used to select the required subject reference, or the entire legal library can be stored. The second method is technically possible but requires a great deal of storage space. The first requires far less storage, but still needs a manual search for the actual information.

But there are methods of concentrating large texts in computer files. For example, to store 20,000,000 words with an average of six characters to each word would take 30,000,000 computer memory locations, assuming four characters could be contained in each location. Such an arrangement would

A search in a conventional library (*top*). A computer search (*bottom*).

require about fifteen magnetic disk storage files. This excessive amount of storage may be reduced by using special codes to represent each word in the text. There may be about 50,000 words used, including verb tenses and inflections, all of which can be represented by a number between 0 and 50,000. Instead of storing actual characters and words, these code numbers can be stored instead. Using this system, we need to store only 20,000,000 *computer* words, plus the code store of 50,000 characters. An additional refinement can be made in systems having large memories by packing two code words into one storage location. In this way, the storage requirements are halved and the system needs only 10,050,000 words of storage.

An advantage of computer filing and indexing systems is that data cannot get missed. Human operators, searching a library for articles on a particular subject, can miss quite a number of references. With a computer system, all the possible references to one subject will be taken from the system files. This accessibility to all information is especially important in law, where a missed reference or prior decision might be sufficiently important to make the difference between winning a case and losing it.

Computers for technical libraries
Closely related to legal information systems are those used to obtain technical information from a library. The number of technical reports and books published doubles about every ten years, producing vast amounts of papers and books on any one subject. Extracting information on a subject from a whole technical library can be assisted by computer indexing. In such a system, the title of each scientific paper is reduced to a number of meaningful words by excluding such words as 'the', 'but', 'and', 'a', and so on. An average of between five and seven words remain, and any one of these can become a *keyword*. In a complete index, the title would appear five to seven times, each time with a different word being used as the key.

For retrieval by computer, information may be punched on a special card (*top*). A blank card is shown (*bottom*).

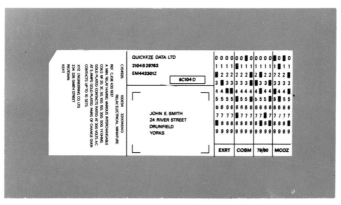

For example, an article called 'An Introduction to Sampled-Data Control Systems' would be reduced to 'Introduction to Sampled Data Controlled Systems'. It has four relevant keywords as follows:

'Introduction to *Sampled* Data Controlled Systems'
'Introduction to Sampled *Data* Controlled Systems'
'Sampled Data Controlled *Systems*, Introduction to'
'Introduction to Sampled Data *Controlled* Systems'.

The keyword 'Introduction' would be considered unnecessary because it has no title-information value. This article would therefore appear four times in the index list.

Although a keyword index can be derived and stored by computer, the search to find relevant articles is still a human function, and will remain so for some time to come. No computer system can decide which titles are relevant to which particular subject. To overcome this, human operators decide which group of articles contain suitable information on a given topic; this bibliography is then stored in a computer, which can produce a list of titles whenever a request is made for information on a particular subject.

Similar indexing and retrieval systems are used for engineers and scientists to enable them to obtain technical product information for their own use. In most technologies, there are thousands of manufacturers producing many different components and specialized pieces of equipment. The object of a *product retrieval system* is to provide the engineer with a list of products and manufacturers of interest in his particular field.

A computer is used to store an up-to-date list of all new and current products in all engineering fields. Each product has a cross-referenced index based on the keyword system, each individual product having a code number and word assigned to it. A group of products for similar applications have a common code letter followed by a type number. An engineer requiring this information uses a similar code letter to indicate his requirements. The computer makes continuous searches of its files, and when the codes coincide, it retrieves data on that product to be sent to the engineer. A punched card is produced containing a printout of the manufacturer and a short description of the component or services offered.

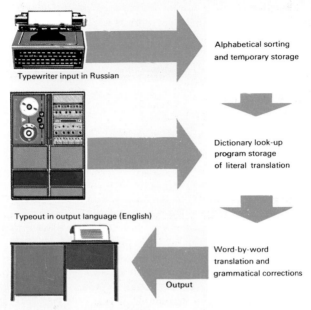

Typewriter input in Russian	Alphabetical sorting and temporary storage
	Dictionary look-up program storage of literal translation
Typeout in output language (English)	Word-by-word translation and grammatical corrections
Output	

A simplified translation system

Computer translation

Automatic language translation by computer has been in use since 1954 and is still being developed as larger and more powerful systems become available. Automatic translation is not as simple as it would first appear, as a pure 'dictionary' translation is of little use. The different rules of word order and grammar in the two languages concerned make the problem very complex. A computer cannot reason and has therefore to translate, by means of fixed rules, from the *input language* into the *output language*. The computer has a record of the grammatical rules of both languages, and a dictionary to convert from input language to output language.

A further problem is that most input words may have several meanings in the output language, so that the true meaning of the particular word can only be determined by examining the rest of the sentence. A human translator does it

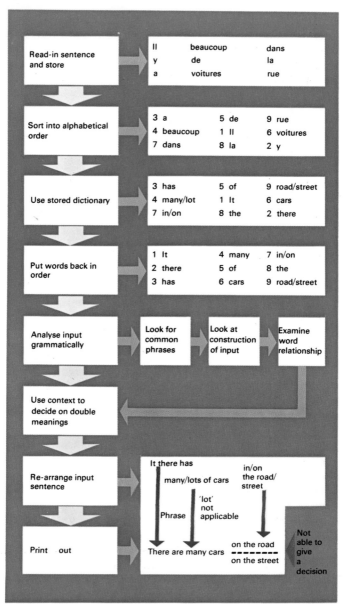

automatically, but a computer cannot use reasoning power to infer meanings in this way. Alternatively, an input word may have a meaning in the input language but no equivalent word in the output language. A human translator would use his judgment in this case to reconstruct the output sentence in such a way as to give the meaning as nearly as possible. A computer, of course, cannot do this directly.

Because of this difficulty, the translated output may not be correct. The 'correctness' of the translation is measured as a percentage – the number of mistakes in a hundred sentences. A 90 per cent translation accuracy is very good by present-day standards, but these figures may be misleading. A sentence may be translated correctly but still not make good sense in the output language, and these sorts of 'mistakes' cannot be measured. Often someone has to correct the computer translation and arrange it into readable form.

A simplified flow diagram is shown on page 106. The sentence to be translated is typed into the computer from a keyboard. In the case of language using special alphabets, such as Russian, a different keyboard must be used. The input language is read into the system and each word in a sentence allocated a number. The sentence is then temporarily stored while a sort program arranges the words into alphabetical order. (This alphabetical sorting is necessary because all the data in the computer dictionary is stored on magnetic tape in alphabetical order. If each word were 'looked up' on the tape in the order it was read-in, the tape storage equipment would be continuously moving backwards and forwards looking for each word in turn, and would take much longer than does passing through the files once in alphabetical order. Exactly similar conditions arise when a human operator has to look up a large number of words in a conventional dictionary.) Once the translation has been made, the sentence is put back into its original order by means of the numbered coding.

The next stage, grammatical analysis, is the most complicated part of the translation process. The rules of syntax and

A flow chart of a computer translation process. Even with this sophisticated approach, a definite decision cannot be made on the exact meaning of the input sentence.

A computer translation centre

grammar for the input language are used to analyse the sentence word by word. All the exceptions, rules, and special expressions or phrases have to be taken into account, and the relationship of any one word to the other words in the sentence examined. Using this information, some decisions on the double meaning of input words may be made, but a memory of all these meanings in different contexts has to be kept. Often, as shown in our example, the computer cannot make a decision as there are no clues in the original sentence to the meaning the writer intended. This can only be solved by examining previous or later sentences; at the moment this is too great a task for even the biggest system.

Factory data retrieval

In large factories using mass-production techniques, much information is needed to enable the manufacturing processes function smoothly. One machine must produce components a given rate in order that the whole production line can run at another rate. To achieve this, stocks of material have to be kept in stores and forecasts of future production have to be estimated. This operation requires a two-way flow of data, from shop floor to a central control point and out again to the shop floor. Then, the control point has instant access to any data and problems are detected, and solved, quickly.

Computers for such systems eliminate the movement of 'written-word' data prepared by office staff. Accurate data is transmitted directly from the shop floor to the computer. Data terminals are placed at strategic points on the factory floor, and information can be fed in from any terminal.

A typical car production data retrieval system is shown on page 111. The complete system not only collects data, but uses it to control the production of the factory.

The sequence of events starts when a customer orders a car or number of cars from a dealer. The dealer then sends a request listing car types, colours, delivery dates, and optional extras to the factory sales department. All this information is coded and fed into the sales computer, which places the order into a pre-planned production schedule and eventually prepares weekly production figures of vehicle types to be fed to the control computer. The sales computer

A data terminal. Operators enter data manually or on punched cards. The computer displays data, when asked, or types-out instructions.

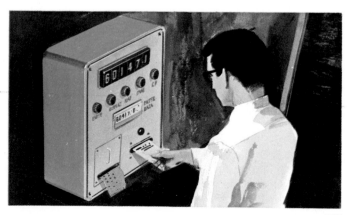

Computers can control all stages in the mass production of cars (*above*). A car factory data retrieval and control system (*right*).

also prepares details of the raw materials needed to meet the latest production forecasts and sends this data to the stores. Meanwhile, the control computer uses the weekly vehicle production figures to prepare detailed instructions for the various machine shops and production lines, on a daily basis. This information is printed-out on a small printer in each data terminal, telling the shop foreman how many of each type of component or assembly to manufacture. As production goes ahead, progress reports are fed back to the computer, informing it of actual production and hold-ups.

Daily production figures are compiled by the control computer for sending to the sales machine. Here, the original production forecasts are modified to suit what is actually happening on the shop floor. This improvement or *optimization* of the factory output enables the best use to be made of all the available manpower and equipment. When the vehicles are finally produced, the dispatch department enters details of the completed cars into the control computer. The computer passes this data on to the sales computer, which takes the finished units off its production schedule. This system then instructs the dispatch department where to send each vehicle and advises the dealer when to expect delivery.

Both computers prepare production and cost information as a management aid for overall planning and control.

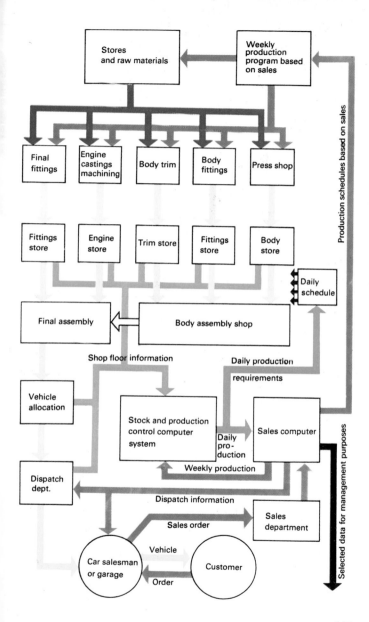

STEEL WORKS

The steel industry has an enormous production output and a wide range of products. For these reasons, controlling a steel works efficiently is a very complicated task, and efforts have been made to apply computers to all aspects of steel production from the preparation of the metal to the making of strips and sheets.

Production control by computer

In any steel works, production must be planned, co-ordinated, and controlled. The diagram on page 114 shows the layout of the production flow of a typical steel works. A central data processing computer receives sales orders for steel. The requirements may be for steel of various shapes (bar, girder, or plate) and of various qualities (such as mild steel or manganese steel). The central computer groups all these orders according to type. For example, all orders for mild steel bar of circular section will be grouped together. As a result, one batch of mild steel can be used to produce all the bar required without changing the rollers on the mills from one cross-section to another. The computer also produces a future loading plan for the works so that all the plant and equipment may be used in the most effective way. This plan may be modified continuously as conditions change. It is used to advise customers of expected delivery dates and to inform the management how the steel works is operating.

In an 'on-line' system, the main computer translates the master plan into individual instructions to process-control computers located at strategic processes. In other systems, the computer prepares all the detailed process instructions.

Once the steel has been made, it is cast into ingots ready for processing. The correct weights of mild steel ingots are then fed into the system, where they are roughly rolled into a slab and the surface scale removed. Shears then cut billets of the required size and weight upon commands from the central computer. Instructions have already been given to the rolling mills to set up the rollers for 2-inch diameter bar production, and the rough billets move into the finishing mills. The

A general view of a steel works

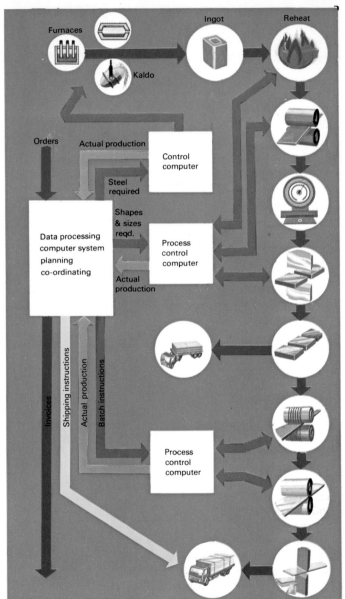

Furnaces

Kaldo

Ingot

Reheat

Orders

Actual production

Control computer

Steel required

Data processing computer system planning co-ordinating

Shapes & sizes reqd.

Process control computer

Actual production

Invoices

Shipping instructions

Actual production

Batch instructions

Process control computer

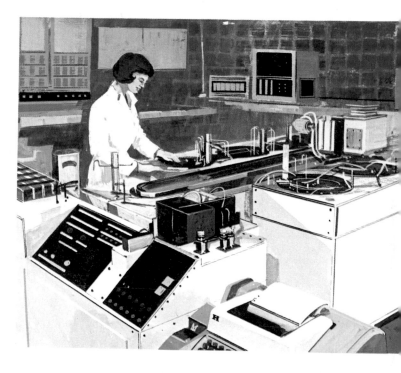

Layout of the production flow of a typical steel works (*left*).
Automatic analysis of steel samples using a computer (*above*).

finished bar is then cut to size, according to requirements,
and left to cool. Instructions are fed by computer to the
dispatch bays to make up the various lengths into consign-
ments for transport and delivery.

Control of shears

Billets and rolled sections are cut by powered shears under
computer control. The shear computer receives instructions
about the required lengths of a given cross-section. As the
billet moves into the mill, the speed of the metal is measured
by photocells, and the computer calculates the speed of the
metal coming out by relating entry speed to the reduction in
cross-section given by the finishing rollers.

The computer consults its file to find the required lengths in sequence, and also calculates the length of moving metal which should be allowed to pass below the shears before sending a signal to operate the shears and cut the metal. The next required length is then allowed to pass before again operating the shears, and so on until the batch is complete.

Controlling a strip mill

Steel strip is essential to many industries. Most is used in making motor cars and much is used by domestic appliance manufacturers.

A steel strip mill rolls strip from thick steel plates or billets produced on the mills described previously. The original plates are about one-tenth of an inch thick and are cold-rolled down to thicknesses of between one-hundredth and seven-hundredths of an inch. A typical mill has four heavy rollers, weighing about five tons each, driven by 5,000 horse-power electric motors. The tension of the rollers can be adjusted to give a pinching force of up to 1,500 tons.

As a plate enters a pair of rollers, it is squeezed down to a thinner cross-section and so it leaves the rollers at a faster speed than it entered. The next roller again squeezes the plate thinner and tensions the strip between the first and second rollers. This process continues until the fourth and final roller, after which an X-ray device measures the thickness of the sheet. A coiler then winds up the sheet into 20-ton rolls. Between each mill, the sheet tension is measured by a roller and a spring-loaded arm arrangement.

A computer can control this process by having in its store a record of all the tensions required to produce a given type of strip of a certain thickness. Each tension-measurer controls the mill roller force directly in advance, and the required tension can be set up by the computer feeding the desired tension into this control loop. If the strip is too thin, the computer slackens off roller A by an amount already recorded in its store. This is followed by instructions to mills B, C, and D to reduce tension, again by a fixed amount as the stored program dictates. Because the computer can work at high speed, the setting-up and control of the mill is far quicker and more efficient than with the manual method.

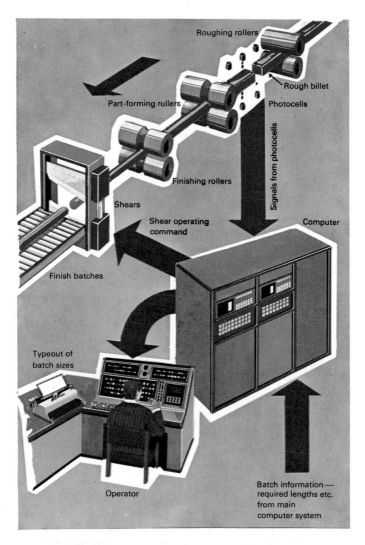

Operating shears by computer. The computer is fed with data on required lengths from a main data processing computer, and calculates the speed of a billet through the first mill from the photocell signals. It then calculates the final length of the billet and arranges the best sizes to be cut from this length.

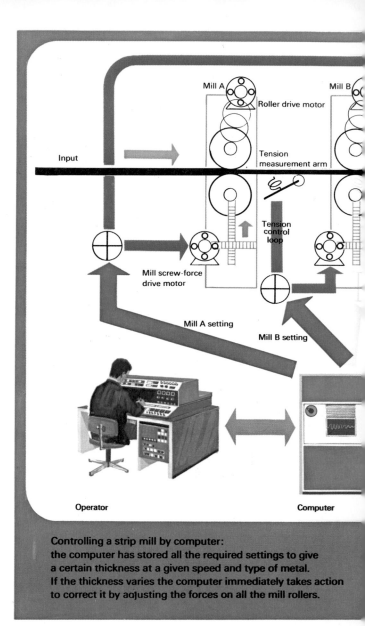

Mill A

Roller drive motor

Mill B

Input

Tension measurement arm

Tension control loop

Mill screw-force drive motor

Mill A setting

Mill B setting

Operator

Computer

Controlling a strip mill by computer:
the computer has stored all the required settings to give
a certain thickness at a given speed and type of metal.
If the thickness varies the computer immediately takes action
to correct it by aojusting the forces on all the mill rollers.

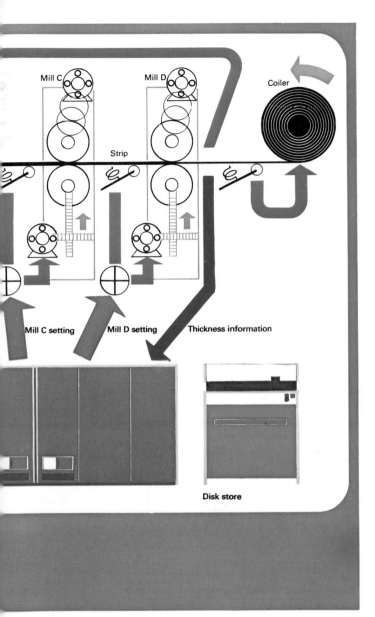

Mill C

Mill D

Coiler

Strip

Mill C setting

Mill D setting

Thickness information

Disk store

119

MESSAGE SWITCHING

An important possible application of a computer is as a kind of 'telephone exchange' to switch and control large amounts of data from different sources. There are two distinct areas in message switching: a computer may be used to read-in a lot of digital data messages from many different sources, sort the data, and send it out over different paths. Or it may be used to recognize where a message is to be routed and set up an 'exchange' path using separate relays or switching circuits to route the actual information-section of the message.

Computer-controlled telephone exchanges

In a conventional telephone exchange, the dialled-in message itself selects the path through the switching system to the required subscriber. The internal wiring of the equipment is

A message-switching computer

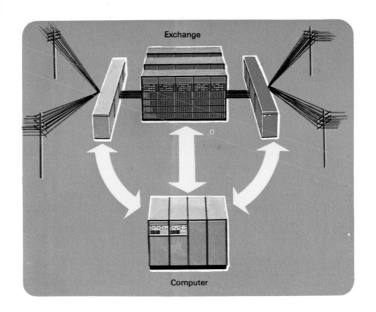

Large telephone exchanges can be controlled by computer.

the 'memory' or record of the action to be taken for any particular dialled request. Whether the subscriber dials a trunk number or a local number, the message is routed by the way in which the exchange is wired.

By controlling the complete exchange by computer, the speed of operation can be increased and the amount of wiring decreased. The computer can store the actions to be taken for any incoming calls and can memorize temporarily the state of the exchange at any time, keeping a record of lines active, and so allocate new lines when required. The computers used for these applications are a *stored-program controlled system*.

When a line becomes active, it may do so for several reasons. A subscriber may have picked up his telephone and be about to dial, a dialling code may be actually coming down the line, a line may be already busy or ringing, and a subscriber may have just finished a call and replaced his handset. If a line is dialling, the computer reads-in the code and decides, from stored-program information, which service is required

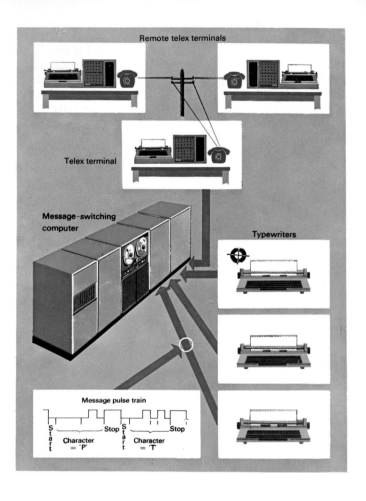

A message-switching computer system. Messages may arrive from either remote telex telegraph stations or typewriters in the same building. Each message contains code numbers indicating its destination, but, before transmission to another remote data terminal, the message is typed-out in the office concerned for modification or approval. The message is then stored, and transmitted together with other messages, when a sufficient number have been assembled to make it economical to do so.

and hence the connections to make. From a previous scan, the computer may have noted a 'busy' signal and if that line is still busy, it will send the 'engaged' signal back to the dialler. Similarly, when a cancelling signal is detected on a particular line, the computer will clear the connections for that line and erase its 'memory' of the call, ready for further calls.

In the design of such equipment, great care has to be taken to ensure that the number of lines used can be *serviced* by the system. If the average rate at which calls arrive in the system exceeds the rate at which the exchange can deal with the calls, a *queue* forms and not all incoming calls can be accepted by the system until the queue is shortened. Fortunately it is very unlikely that everyone connected to an exchange will dial at the same time, and the equipment need be designed to handle only a small number of the total possible messages at the same time. This number has to be carefully chosen, using the mathematical theories of probabilities. In modern systems, the switching network uses fast-acting *reed relays.* These relays are small switches consisting of spring-steel 'reeds' sealed in a glass tube. When externally magnetized, the reeds move together and make contact. These switches take about only two milliseconds to close and one millisecond to open, making possible very fast connection speeds.

Switching computer messages

When small numbers of lines (about 200) need to be switched in digital form, the computer can itself act as the switching network. This application is ideal for linking together large numbers of teleprinters or typewriters in offices and factories. The computer operates so quickly compared to the input that it can read-in, sort, and output messages entirely by itself.

Most communication lines carry teleprinter or type-writer messages as *serial data,* which are groups of pulses called *bits* representing characters and sent along the lines. These pulses are only twenty milliseconds long and each character may be made up of ten bits, so that each character takes 200 milliseconds to send. This represents a typing speed of five characters per second. If 100 such lines are fed to a computer system, it may only take five microseconds to sample a line to see if it is carrying a pulse, so that all the

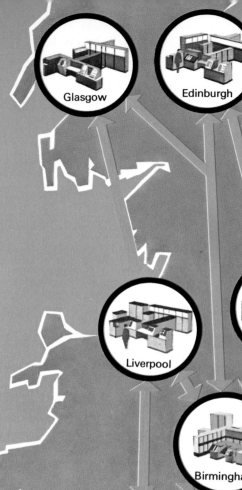

Glasgow

Edinburgh

Liverpool

Leeds

Birmingham

Bristol

London

lines can be sampled in 500 microseconds. As a result, each line is sampled at 500-microsecond intervals, and each 20-millisecond pulse could be sampled forty times at this speed.

This line-sampling task is often performed by a device, separate from the computer, called a *multi-channel controller*. It not only samples all the lines in turn, but also collects the information coming in until such time as enough data has been gathered to transfer it all at high speed into the computer. Thus computing time is not wasted by bringing in single lines.

In a typical message-switching system, the characters are transferred into the memory directly as a mixture of channel numbers and characters, as they come in. Each memory location consists of one character and the channel number upon which the character came in. A sorting program then assembles these random characters into messages from each channel, and outputs the channel on a line like the input system.

This sort of system can be expanded into a versatile business accessory. In addition to being switched, a message may be introduced into the system from telex or teleprinter lines on the normal telephone network. By using magnetic disks or tapes, messages may be stored and modified.

Large international business offices use such systems. Incoming telex messages, perhaps from overseas, are identified by a code number for transmission to a given office. After passing through the message switch, the message is typed-out in the office concerned and then may be modified or have comments added before being re-transmitted to its destination. The message-switching computer can store many messages for one telex or teleprinter destination until such time as it is economical to transmit large amounts of data.

Linked computers
The idea of a national computer grid has been popular for a number of years. In such a grid, many computers all over the country would be linked by high-speed telegraph or radio-telephone paths. Information stored in a computer in,

The idea of a 'computer grid'. Systems in major cities would be linked by high-speed telephone lines and any system would have access to the files or computing power of other systems.

say, Leeds could be used by a system in Edinburgh, and vice versa. Also spare computing time on one computer installation would be available for use by a heavily loaded installation elsewhere.

The drawback of normal telephone lines is that they are limited to a data transfer rate between installations of about 2,000 bits a second. Modern radio-telephone or high-frequency cable links can increase this speed to 40,000 bits a second, a speed which is much nearer computer speeds.

To establish a computer grid will require highly involved programming techniques. A common code or *language* must be agreed for all the system to use.

In the future, even more complex systems are envisaged. A research worker in London may require data from a system in Birmingham. Such systems will make use of *message concentrators* to achieve this type of personal contact. A personal request would be given from a normal typewriter keyboard and perhaps CRT display. For the whole London system, a single typewriter keyboard would take far too much time to read-in because the message would be so slow. Other people may also be typing-in to the system and take up even more of the large system's time. A message concentrator is used to compress such slow data into a very short, fast burst which the large system will take very little time to read-in.

For example, suppose a typewriter is sending in a message of 120 characters at a speed of five characters a second. This message takes twenty-five seconds for the large computer to read-in. If concentrated, it would take as little as 600 microseconds, about 40,000 times as fast. Savings in time would be even greater if many slow inputs were connected to the same message concentrator.

The London system could then quickly assess the data and send the original request over the high-speed link to the Birmingham system, where the reverse process occurs. The large system will process the incoming request and extract the relevant information from its files. If the request is made to an individual, it will pass through a message concentrator to the relevant typewriter. In this case, the message concentrator slows down the high-speed information from the main system to a suitable speed for typing-out.

126

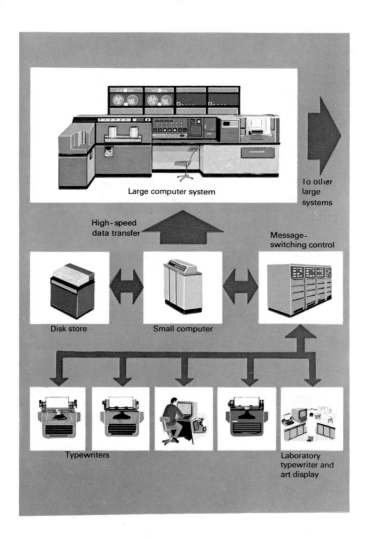

Large computer system

To other large systems

High-speed data transfer

Message-switching control

Disk store

Small computer

Typewriters

Laboratory typewriter and art display

A message concentrator. The large system's time is very expensive and so it would be uneconomical for it to waste time reading-in slow-speed lines. A smaller and cheaper system reads-in these lines and stores data until complete messages are formed. The messages are then transmitted at very high speed to the large computer.

6.45 pm: 4 May 1968: owner reports theft of car. Police sergeant answering phone immediately types on remote console of regional computer (25 miles away):

STOLEN CAR NO XYZ 123 BLUE FORD ANGLIA. SHARTON 1845.

20 minutes later: policeman in Minchester (in the next county) sees a car entering a suspect garage. He radios description to Minchester control room where operator types on console connected to same regional computer:

CAR NO XYZ 123 BLUE FORD ANGLIA SEEN MIN-CHESTER 1905.

Within seconds, the regional computer (50 miles away) prints simultaneously on its own printer and on the Minchester control room console:

XYZ 123 BLUE FORD ANGLIA STOLEN SHARTON 1845 4/5/68.

7.06 pm: within a minute of their enquiry, the mobile police get their reply and orders. They investigate the garage.

7.15 pm:
search reveals a blue Ford Anglia but its number is 789 ABC. Radio message to control room. Operator types on console:

CAR NO 789 ABC BLUE FORD ANGLIA SEEN MINCHESTER 1915.

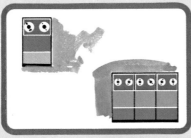

1 second later:
regional computer prints out:

789 ABC NOT KNOWN. NATIONAL RECORD SOUGHT.

Two minutes later:
national computer responds to regional computer after looking up in complete records. Message passed on to Minchester control room:

789 ABC BLACK FORD ANGLIA BODY NUMBER 100E/9251 REGISTERED TO P. BROWN, LONDON ROAD, SHARTON.

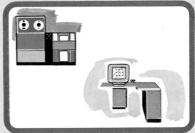

7.25 pm:
Body number does not check; it is 100E/7186. Enquiry to national computer reveals 5 minutes later that this body number belongs to XYZ 123.

Collapse (and arrest) of stout party who turns out to be P. Brown!

POLICE RECORDS OF CARS

Records of various kinds are extremely important to the police in all aspects of their work, and computers can help them in many ways. In this chapter, we shall be concerned with the way in which computers can help to speed police enquiries by storing information about motor vehicles.

There are three main situations in which the police require to be able to trace a vehicle urgently: when a vehicle has been stolen, when it is suspected that a vehicle is being used by a criminal, and when there has been a hit-and-run accident involving injury or death. There are also several other situations in which the police require information about vehicles, but less urgently. They may wish to trace cars found abandoned, cars observed committing parking offences, and cars involved in accidents not resulting in injury.

The computer system will consist of one large national computer storing the registration records of all vehicles in the country. This central computer will communicate with several regional computers that store the more transient information about local criminals and local accidents. The regional computers, in turn, connect with automatic typewriter consoles in the main police stations of the area.

The records in the central computer would be of three types: the national list of all motor vehicles; a register of all vehicles reported stolen in the country; and a copy of all the local lists of vehicles associated with known offenders.

The records in the local computers would also be of three types. The first would be an exact copy of the national list of stolen vehicles, the second would be a list of vehicles used by known criminals and their associates or by disqualified drivers in that region, and the third would be a list of vehicles registered in the region and suspected of being involved in hit-and-run accidents.

A typical urgent enquiry might arise when a police car observes another car behaving suspiciously. The police observer in his car would send a radio message to the control

A computer system could help to trace cars reported stolen (*pages 128–129*) or cars involved in accidents (*right*).

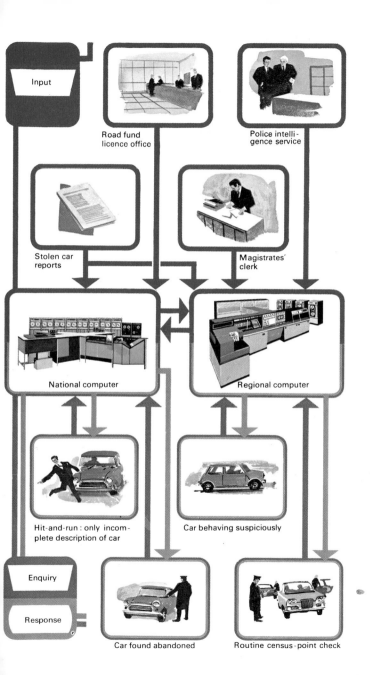

Input

Road fund
licence office

Police intelli-
gence service

Stolen car
reports

Magistrates'
clerk

National computer

Regional computer

Hit-and-run : only incom-
plete description of car

Car behaving suspiciously

Enquiry

Response

Car found abandoned

Routine census-point check

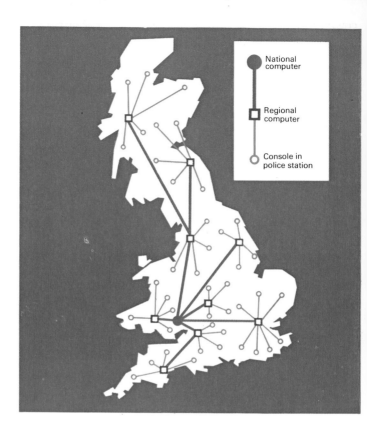

Layout of a projected police intelligence system

room, asking whether the suspect car's registration number was on the local list of cars known to the police. The answer to this query would come back very quickly. If it was not on the list, the police car would do nothing. But the computer would record the information for reference.

The enquiry from the control room to the computer would be made by a police officer who would type on the console keyboard the relevant registration number, with a code message indicating the urgency of the enquiry. The regional computer would indicate within seconds whether or not that registration number was on one of the local active records. If it was, the computer would send the relevant information to be printed-out by the typewriter in the control room.

An incomplete description of a car, for example its make, colour, and part of its registration number, might be provided by a witness of a hit-and-run accident. If the accident was serious, the police would wish to get from the national computer a list of all the cars registered in the neighbourhood that answered this partial description. This information could be obtained by sending a message from the console in the police station to the national computer via the regional computer. The national computer would contain a program allowing it to search parts of the national record for relevant combinations of particulars. The program would instruct the machine to look first for cars registered in the locality of the accident, and would try all registration numbers fitting the partially remembered particulars.

Diagram showing local police communications

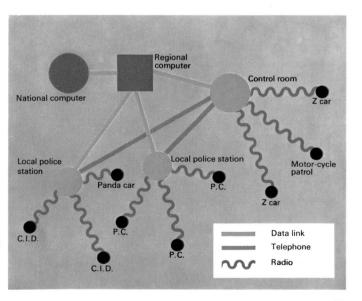

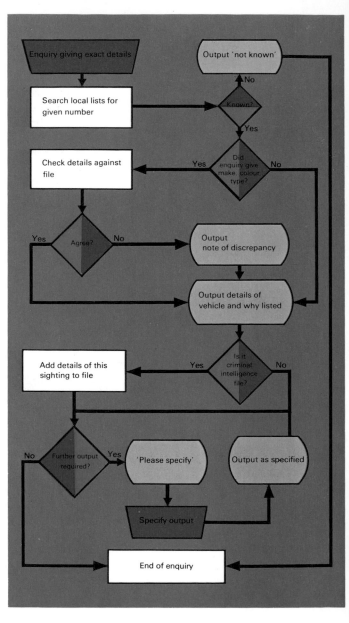

If there were only a few suspect cars in the locality, say up to 100, this list could be added to the list of cars known to the police locally, and eliminated from it as police visits or other enquiries cleared them from the list of suspects.

The important feature of both the national and the local computers in this system would be their capability of time-sharing, which means that they could handle enquiries from, and responses to, a number of consoles at the same time. The regional computer would probably be connected to twenty or thirty consoles in police stations, and the national computer might well be connected to several hundred. On the regional level, it would be essential that no police station should be kept waiting because another one was making an enquiry. This could be done by making use of the fact that the computer can work very much faster than a typewriter (1,000,000 operations per second compared with about fifteen characters per second): if a number of typewriters are connected to a computer, it is possible to allocate a proportion of the operations in any one second to each typewriter.

Flow chart for enquiry 'Is this car known locally?' (*left*). Samples of console typewriter printout (*below*): input typed by police officer (*left*) and output typed under remote control (*right*).

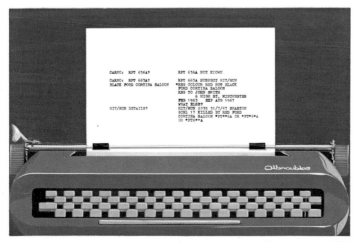

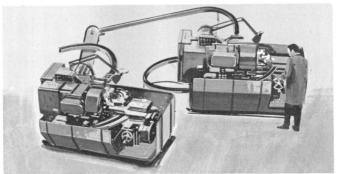

Automatic machine tools : chuck and turret arrangement of automatic lathe (*top*), computer-controlled lathes (*bottom*).

DESIGN AUTOMATION

For several years, automatic machine tools have been used for manufacturing small components in large quantities. In this way, lathe and milling-machine operators may be transferred from repetitive jobs to do more exacting work. In a *milling* operation, the workpiece (metal to be machined) is moved up or down, left or right, or backwards or forwards under a tool, such as a rotating cutter. With manual working of these machines, an operator controls the movement of the workpiece clamped to the milling-machine 'bed' or table in such a way that the desired shape is machined.

In a digital computer control system, the table and work-piece are moved the required amounts by means of signals sent to vertical, horizontal, or transverse motors. These signals are pre-recorded on magnetic or punched tape, which can be rewound after one item is completed, ready for the next workpiece. There are several methods of achieving this control. One method uses optical equipment which generates an electrical pulse for each quarter-thousandth of an inch movement of the workpiece in the three planes. By electronically counting these pulses, the computer can issue signals to drive the workpiece to a given position. Another system works on an *incremental* principle, in which special drive-motors move on a fixed amount every time a pulse is given. Such motors drive the three movements of the workpiece.

To cut a straight line in a workpiece on the table, the longitudinal drive-motor needs to receive pulses at a fixed rate to drive the work under the cutter at a fixed speed. The faster the pulses are, the faster is the cutting rate.

If both transverse and longitudinal drives are 'pulsed' at the same speed, an angled cut is made. And by varying the

Computer-controlled drilling machine

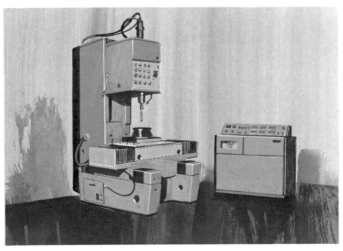

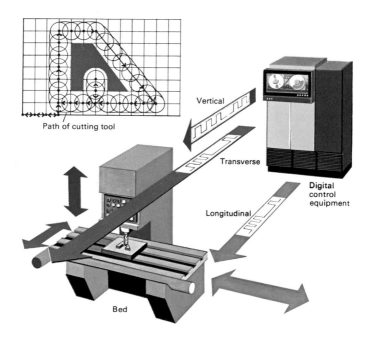

Vertical

Transverse

Digital control equipment

Longitudinal

Bed

Path of cutting tool

Basic machining operations

two drive-rates according to the correct mathematical relationship, a circular drive can be pulsed to vary the depth of the cut or to disengage the tool from the workpiece.

All the pulses for the three motors can be recorded on magnetic tape. The problem is how to get the right pulses, in the correct sequences and relationship to each other, onto the tape. To do this, use is made of the computer and a machine-tool *control language*.

The machine-tool control program also sets up the correct sequence of pulses for certain shapes and materials. For example, if a machine is to cut a straight line between two points, the instructions in the input language need only define the starting point and end point of the line and the computer program generates all the pulses required to move the workpiece between these two points. The speed of cutting is also given in the input language, which generates the corresponding pulses at the correct rate.

Such programming may take a long time and have to be frequently tested on trial workpieces made of plastic. But once the program has been perfected, it can be used for mass production. In a fully automated system, the magnetic tape also controls the ejection of the finished component, clamping of the new workpiece, and rewinding of the tape.

Automatic drawing

Instead of a work table being moved under a tool, a pen may be made to move over the surface of a sheet of paper. Connected to a computer, such a device can trace curves and shapes using simple instructions in an input language.

Such systems are used for plotting large templates in sheet metal working, and for drawing cam profiles. Use has also

A computer can prepare drawings of any new design.

been made of these drawing aids in the micro-electronics industry. Micro-circuits are used in most modern computers and are manufactured by etching out or diffusing materials into small pieces of silicon using various masks which outline the shape of the circuit. The masks are extremely small and must be made by optical reduction from very large master drawings to obtain the required accuracy. Computers can calculate the best layouts and draw the required masks.

Future developments

In the future, a computer system might completely design *and* manufacture components. The component to be made can be 'drawn' onto the surface of a CRT display by means of a light-pen connected to a computer. The display scans the whole face of the tube under computer control, and when the light-pen is brought near to the surface of the tube it receives a small 'flash' of light as the scanning beam passes it. At this

Drawing by computer

The activities of several units can be controlled by specially prepared tapes made by the computer above.

instant, a signal or 'interrupt' is sent from the light-pen to the computer which remembers the position on the screen which the beam scanned when the pen gave an interrupt. This procedure continues as the operator moves the pen over the screen, and eventually a complete trace of all the points is constructed. In this way, an operator can 'draw' the required component and then enter its dimensions into the system from a normal keyboard. The computer then constructs the trains of pulses required to machine the shape automatically.

This data is then put onto magnetic tape which can later be transferred to the machine-tool control equipment. There is no reason why many machines should not be programmed by the designs produced by one computer system, so reducing the time required for an operator to work out by hand all the required component dimensions.

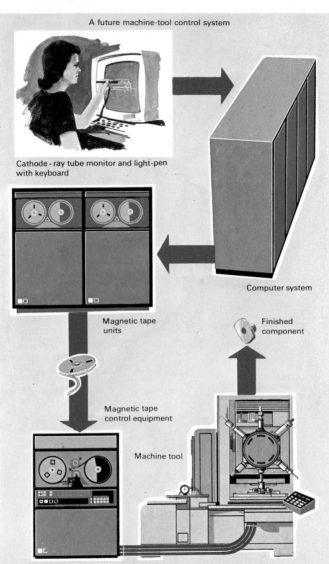

A future machine-tool control system

Cathode-ray tube monitor and light-pen with keyboard

Computer system

Magnetic tape units

Finished component

Magnetic tape control equipment

Machine tool

The operator 'draws' the required component and dimensions it from his keyboard. The computer allocates machine movements to copy the shape and puts this information onto magnetic tape. Opposite: complex computer-controlled machine tools.

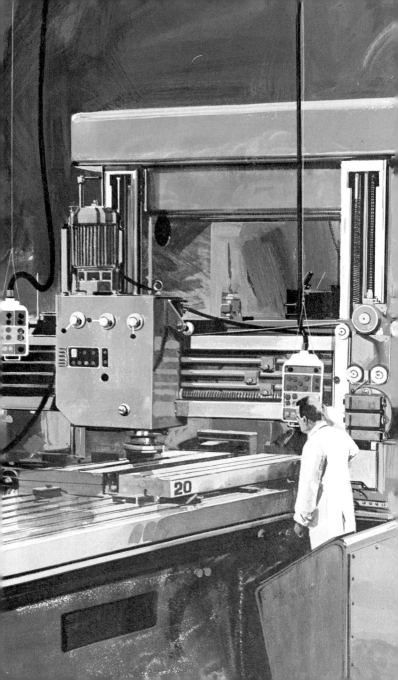

FREIGHT TERMINALS

Containerization is one of the most exciting developments in modern freight transport. By using a standard-sized container, small loose goods may be carried in fixed units by road, rail, sea, or air. As more countries adopt the system, an integrated international freight transportation system will result, giving a more rapid and efficient method of moving goods from country to country.

The aspects of organization with container freight that perhaps require the greatest attention are the terminal depots. At these, containers are transferred from one means of transportation to another, for example ship to lorry or railway and vice versa, and lorry to railway or aircraft and vice versa. Terminals have to handle large numbers of containers of various weights and sizes and intended for different destinations.

In this chapter, we shall look at an ocean terminal, as this type caters for the greatest numbers of containers at once and for several kinds of transport. Container ships have special holds in which containers are stacked in such a way that a crane can always gain access to any part of the hold. The

A ship at a freight terminal being loaded with containers by a computer-controlled loader (*below*). Loader removing container from lorry (*right*).

144

containers can be loaded and unloaded entirely by using automatic handling equipment.

Even with the most modern automated container ships and expensive lifting gear, and with lorries and trains efficiently moving containers between factories and the jetty, the whole system loses its effectiveness if the container is not at the quayside at the right time. It is here that the computer can speed the flow of goods and provide a quick turnround, using both ships and port facilities to their maximum extent.

A computer can provide several services for an ocean terminal installation. It can calculate the best way to fit a number of containers of different weights and sizes into a ship so as to keep the vessel in trim and utilize all the available space to the best advantage. A computer can also, having done this, route each lorry to the quayside so that it arrives there at the correct time for its container to be loaded onto the ship. Instructions are given to the crane driver, telling him where in the ship to stack or unload each container. If a container does not arrive in time for loading, the computer can rapidly calculate a new way to stack the containers in the hold using the containers that *are* available. Very few lorries will arrive at the terminal exactly at the correct time to be loaded or unloaded, and the computer can arrange and route them through the terminal in the quickest possible way.

The diagram on page 149 is a plan of a typical dock installation. For the purposes of computer engineering, it is best to

Container lorry at docks (*below*). Layout showing typical control functions performed by computer system (*right*).

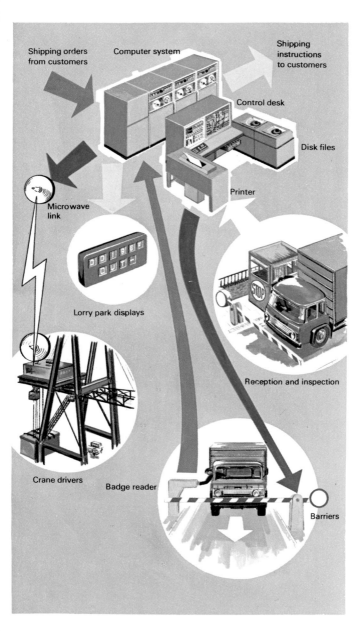

Shipping orders from customers

Computer system

Shipping instructions to customers

Control desk

Disk files

Printer

Microwave link

Lorry park displays

Reception and inspection

Crane drivers

Badge reader

Barriers

consider that the ocean terminal is a 'system' in itself with an input and output of lorries, either empty or loaded.

A customer orders shipments in advance, and specifies the numbers of containers with their sizes, weights, code numbers, and destinations. The details of all the containers for one destination are grouped together ready for one ship and stored in advance on the computer's files. When this data has been assembled, the different shipping dates are compared and suitable times for dispatching containers are worked out and sent to the various customers.

When lorries arrive at the terminal, some may be picking up containers being unloaded. The layout of containers in the ship's hold and their code-number information are radioed ahead of the ship when it leaves its previous port, and this data is fed into the computer. As a lorry enters the 'system', it is held at the reception gate while the operator there types into the computer details of the container's code number, weight, and size. Or if it is an empty lorry, he types the code number of the container to be collected. At the reception point, the lorry driver is given a punched and numbered card which will identify his lorry until he leaves the system.

Having read-in this data, the computer examines its files to see if the load arriving tallies with its own information about this particular cargo. If it does, the computer examines its store to see if a crane is immediately available to deal with the load, and if it is, it raises the barrier to allow the lorry to the 'stack' on the quayside. If the crane is busy, the computer again examines its store to see if there is room in the quayside lorry park for the lorry to wait until it is called for. If neither of these courses is possible, the lorry is directed to the main lorry park to wait for room in the quayside park, when it is then called on.

When room is available in the quayside lorry park, the computer 'calls' the next lorry by displaying the lorry code number and instructions where to go on a large display in

The efficiency of a freight terminal for handling containerized goods depends on the smooth and controlled flow of containers on and off the quayside. Incoming lorries take one of three routes: straight to the quay, to the quayside lorry park, or to the main park.

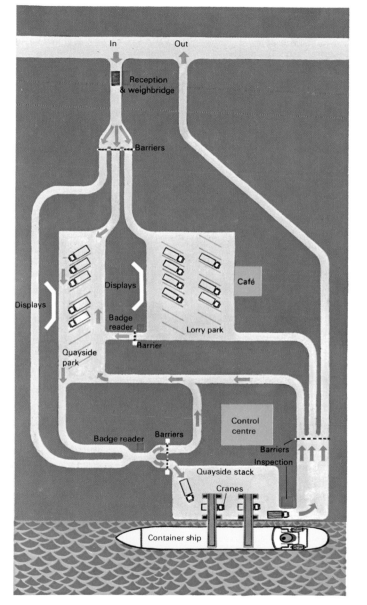

the main lorry car park. The lorry driver gives details of his container at the barrier into the quayside park by putting his plastic badge into a card reader at the side of the road. The computer recognizes this and raises the barrier to allow the load to pass.

As the crane becomes free, the next lorry number is displayed in the quayside park and the lorry moves off to the quay barrier. Here the driver again identifies his container, and if all is correct, the barrier giving access to the 'stack' rises. If an error has occurred and the wrong lorry has arrived at the badge reader, the barrier leading back into the quayside park is opened.

The lorry now moves to the next available crane, whose driver has been informed, by means of a typewriter operating over a microwave link, where in the ship to put the next load. After unloading, the lorry moves to the inspection barrier where all of the relevant data about that lorry is re-entered into the computer. If all is well and the container loaded, the driver returns his badge and the computer raises the exit barrier; the lorry has now left the system. If, however, the flow of containers has got out of order, the computer may instruct the lorry back into the system, either to return to the quayside park or to the main lorry park.

Exactly the same flow of lorries occurs when a ship is unloading. The computer already has a list of containers for unloading and will instruct the crane driver which containers to unload, starting at the tops of the holds. At the same time, the computer calls the lorry concerned to the quayside for loading. As the lorry leaves, the load is checked to see whether it corresponds to the information punched onto the badge issued to the driver, and if so, the lorry leaves the system as before.

After a ship is completely loaded, the actual cargo may differ from the one originally stored by the computer because some loads have not arrived. The computer notes the differences and produces a typeout which gives details of the layout and coding of all the containers in the ship. This list is then transmitted to the container ship's next port of call.

Flow chart for container handling

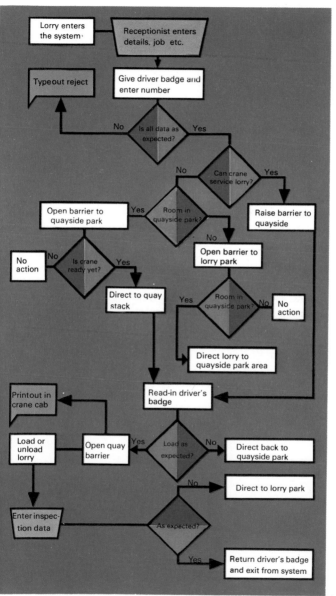

Lorry enters the system · → Receptionist enters details, job etc. → Give driver badge and enter number → **Is all data as expected?** — No → Typeout reject

Is all data as expected? — Yes → **Can crane service lorry?**

Can crane service lorry? — Yes → Raise barrier to quayside

Can crane service lorry? — No → **Room in quayside park?**

Room in quayside park? — Yes → Open barrier to quayside park → **Is crane ready yet?**

Room in quayside park? — No → Open barrier to lorry park → **Room in quayside park?** — Yes → Direct lorry to quayside park area

Room in quayside park? — No → No action

Is crane ready yet? — No → No action

Is crane ready yet? — Yes → Direct to quay stack → Read-in driver's badge

Read-in driver's badge → **Load as expected?**

Load as expected? — Yes → Open quay barrier → Load or unload lorry

Load as expected? — No → Direct back to quayside park

Open quay barrier → Printout in crane cab

Load or unload lorry → Enter inspection data → **As expected?**

As expected? — No → Direct to lorry park

As expected? — Yes → Return driver's badge and exit from system

CONCLUSION

It has been said in this book that a computer could perform certain tasks if only it could be made large enough. When those words were written, the transistorized computer was already well established, but development of the silicon chip integrated circuit was still to come.

Paradoxically, silicon chip technology not only enables us to make much larger computers, because so much complex circuitry is packed into so little space, but it has also opened the way to the mass production of much smaller computers.

A typical silicon chip measures 0.1 in × 0.15 in, though its mount, with its array of connecting pins, is necessarily much bigger. To give an idea of what the chip achieves for us in terms of space saving, we have only to realize that by 1977 a single-program memory chip with a 2,048 bit capacity replaces 13–25-generation integrated circuits which, in turn, had replaced between 125–256 logic 'gates' of the original computers of the 1960s.

The commercial merit of chip technology lies in mass-production through standardization. The computer process is broken down into its four basic functions, for which there is a 'family' of four chips. These are the *central processing*

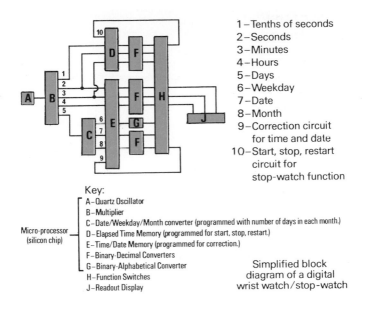

1 – Tenths of seconds
2 – Seconds
3 – Minutes
4 – Hours
5 – Days
6 – Weekday
7 – Date
8 – Month
9 – Correction circuit
for time and date
10 – Start, stop, restart
circuit for
stop-watch function

Key:

Micro-processor (silicon chip)

A – Quartz Oscillator
B – Multiplier
C – Date/Weekday/Month converter (programmed with number of days in each month.)
D – Elapsed Time Memory (programmed for start, stop, restart.)
E – Time/Date Memory (programmed for correction.)
F – Binary-Decimal Converters
G – Binary-Alphabetical Converter
H – Function Switches
J – Readout Display

Simplified block
diagram of a digital
wrist watch / stop-watch

unit (CPU); the *read-write memory* (RWM); the *read-only memory* (ROM); and an *input/output* chip which enables connection of the CPU to keyboards, displays, outside memory banks, line printers and other peripheral devices.

Quantity production is feasible, with attendant cost savings, because all CPUs, RWMs and input/output chips in a particular manufacturer's family are identical, being designed for use either singly or ganged up in multiple arrays. The ROM, which is designed to store an operating program, is manufactured for a customer's particular purpose. As its name implies, it holds a program which can be read but not altered. While custom-produced, this is achieved by a relatively inexpensive mask programming process.

The simplest computer, known as a micro-processor, need have just two chips: one ROM and one CPU, since the latter includes its own small memory section and a basic input/output system. At the other end of the scale, the latest silicon chips

Left: The pencil indicates the small size of a silicon chip. This ITT 4116 chip (16K RAM) measures 0.23in. by 0.14in.

can be built into larger and larger arrays, which have immense computing power packed into relatively small space. For example, a high-speed micro-processor magnetic disk controller can operate a rapid access 400 megabit memory bank using 67 chips wired neatly into a single 8 in × 15 in circuit board, replacing what would formerly have been a relatively clumsy network of 200 or more integrated circuits.

The micro-processor has also opened up the technology for use in almost every walk of life where an electronic 'brain' can be useful, but where the physical size of the unit formerly made this impracticable. The most obvious example is the digital watch, in which a micro-processor multiplies the vibrations of a quartz crystal to produce hundredths of a

Above: A desk computer, of the kind manufactured by International Computers Limited, used by such organizations as building societies for rapid checking of account details.

second (in the stop-watch facility), seconds, minutes, hours and days. An ROM section keeps track of the differing days in each month, converts days into both dates by number and weekdays by name, and an RAM section retains the precise time as well as the elapsed time while the stop-watch function is in use. Finally, an input/output circuit connects the processor to display and to the tiny switches with which the time is set, via the ROM, and the stop-watch function operated.

The inevitable conclusion is that while there is still far to go, computer technology is advancing rapidly in the direction of being able to pack the intelligence of a human brain into a man-made package that could be man handled.

Left: Computer systems controlled by the human voice — or 'voice recognition systems' — have a wide range of applications. The quality inspector here is checking a TV faceplate for accuracy of size. Direct voice input of his findings speeds interaction with the computer. The speaker has 'trained' the machine to understand his speaking of a vocabulary of words, numbers, or short phrases, and a 'pattern' for each vocabulary word is stored as the computer's reference memory pattern. The patterns for several speakers can be held simultaneously.

BOOKS TO READ

For general introductions to the subject of computers and their uses, the following recently published books are recommended. They are generally available from bookshops and public libraries.

The Computer Age by M. Campbell-Kelly. Wayland, London, 1978.

Computers and Commonsense (2nd edition) by Roger Hunt. Prentice-Hall, London, 1979.

Electronic Computers (Rev. 3rd edition) by S. H. Hollingdale. Pelican, London, 1975.

Introduction to Microprocessors by David Aspinall. Pitman, London, 1977.

Introduction to On-Line Systems by J. A. T. Pritchard. National Computer Centre Publications, 1973.

An Introduction to the Uses of Computers by Murray Laver. Cambridge University Press, London, 1976.

Minicomputers and Microprocessors by Martin Healey. Hodder Educational, London, 1976.

A Short History of Computers (2nd edition) by A. J. Sly. Advisory Council for Computer-Based Education, Hertfordshire County Council, 1976.

Your Book of Computers by K. N. Dodd. Faber, London, 1969.

INDEX

Page numbers in bold type refer to
illustrations.

Accounts 22
Active measurement 16
Activity 6
ADC *see* Analog-to-digital converter
Air crew 56
Air traffic 64
Aircraft 12, 15, **15,** 56
Aircraft emergency 76
Aircraft maintenance 71
Aircraft movement order 69, 74, **74,** 76
Aircraft servicing **62,** 71
Airlines 52, **54**
Airspeed 13
Alarm 37
Analog signal 37
Analog-to-digital converter 14, **36,** 37,
90
Antenna control **13**
Anticyclone 80
Apollo 16
Archives 56
Atomic clock 16
Atomic physics 91
Automatic drawing 139
Automatic pilot 12, 13
Automatic wiring **94,** 95, **95, 96**
Automation 136
medical 84

Balloon **78,** 79, **79**
Banking 18, 22, **23**
Bearings 16
Bibliography 104
Binary number 37
Bit 97, 123
Blood pressure 86
Blood test 84
Boiler 35
Booking **67,** 86
Buffer register 29
Buffer store 38
Bulk storage 40
Business transactions 21

Calendar program 40
Car production 109, **111**
Card reader **18, 20,** 22, **57, 59,** 62, 86,
109, 150
Cathode-ray tube 38, **39,** 61, **61**
Central processor 95, 152
Cheque 22
Circuit testing 98
Clearing house 22

Closed-circuit television 28
Code 102, 127
Colour television **90, 91**
Computer
analog 4, 12, 13, 44, **45, 90,** 92
checkout 16, 98
control 29
digital 4, 14, **44,** 45, 137
manufacture of 95
message 28, **28**
portable 16, **154**
speed of 43
Computer grid **124,** 125
Computer power supply 43
Container ship 146
Containerization 144, **151**
Control language 138
Core 97
Core store 56, **57,** 59
Cost of computer equipment 58
Credit card 66
Crew roster 73
Critical path 5, 6, **6,** 7, 8, **8, 10,** 11
CRT *see* Cathode-ray tube

Data 4, 42
Data communications 84
Data links 22
Data processing **36,** 84, **114**
Data retrieval 108, **111**
Data terminal **18,** 22, **23,** 109, **109, 122**
Data transmission 127
Decision point 31
Design automation 136
Diagnosis 92, **93**
Dialling 40, 121
Dictionary 105, **105**
Digital signal 37
Digital watch **153,** 154
Disks, speed of 60
Disk pack 60, 61
Disk store 4, **19,** 56, **57,** 59, **60,** 102, 125
Display 28, **31, 32, 33, 34, 36,** 38, **39,**
42, **53, 57,** 58, 61, **61,** 84, **109,** 127, 140,
142, 148
speed of 38
Docks 146, **149**
Doctor 92
Drawing 139, **139, 140**
Drilling machine **137**
Drum store 4, **36,** 40, 42
Duplication 15

ECG *see* Electrocardiograph
Editing 46
EEC *see* Electroencephalograph
Electricity supply **34,** 35, 44

Electrocardiograph 84, 86, **87**, 88, **93**
Electroencephalograph 86, **87**
Electronic clock 40
Event 7
Executive program 40

Factory 108
Filing 102
Filmsetting 51
Finance 18
Flight engineer 13
Flight schedule 56, 64
Float 9, 11
Flow chart 64
Freight terminal 144, **144, 149**

Gamma camera **90**, 92
Graph plotter **44**
Grammar 108
Grid 44

Hardware 5, 56
Hard-copy 56, 58, 62
Heart waveform 86, 88, 91
Histogram 9
Hospitals 84—92
Hospital bed allocation 86
Hospital theatre allocation 86
Hybrid system 45
Hyphenation 47, 48

Incremental drive 137
Incremental plotter 80
Indexing 101, 102, 104
Induction-loop detector 26
Information retrieval 101, **103**
Input 4, 152
Input language 105, 107, 108
Insurance 18
Integrated circuit 14, 152
Intensive-care 86, **87**
Interrupt **40**
Interrupt system 37
Isotope 91

Justification 47

Keyboard **5**, 107, 141
Keypunch **59**
Keyword 102, 104

Land-line 56
Language 107, 108, 127, 138
Lathe **136**
Law 101
Legal library 101

Letters, formation of 38
Library **100**, 101
Light-pen 140, **142**
Line breaks 48
Line printer 4, **18, 44, 46, 57, 78**
Linotype machine 51
Logic 95
Logic function 98

Machine tools 136—141, **142**
Magnetic drum see Drum store
Magnetic store 38
Magnetic tape **5**, 45, **87, 90,** 125, 137
138, 141, **142**
Main-frame 95
Manuscript 46, 47
Mass production 108, **110**
Matrix 97
Medical library 92
Medicine 84
Memory 4, 42, 86, 88, 95, 97, **97**, 98, 125
capacity of 40
Memory testing 98
Message concentrator **23, 126,** 127
Message switching 58, 120, **120, 122,**
125
Meteorology 79
Micro-circuit **99**
Micro-electronics 140
Micro-processor 152, **153,** 154
Milling 136, **136**
Missile 15
Modem **57,** 58
Money 18
Monitoring 42
Motor accident 130, **131**
Multi-channel controller 125
Multiplexer **34,** 37, 88
Multiprocessor 58, 84

National grid 44, **44**
Navigation 12, **12,** 13, 16, 17
Navigator 14
Network 6, 7
Nuclear power station 35
Nursing 84

Off-line 61
On-line 22, 84
Operational mode 37
Optimization 110
Orbits 17
Output 4, 152
Output language 105, 107

Page setting 51
Panel processing program 42
Payrolls 18
Photocell 115, **117**

Photosetting 51
Pilot 73
Police records 130, **131**
Policeman 24
Power failure 43
Power station 35, **35**, **43**
Pressure pad **24**, 26
Printed circuits **94**, 95, 98
Printing 46–51
Printout **5**, 104
Priority interrupt 40, 42
Processor 29, 56
Product retrieval 104
Production control 113
Program 4, 37, 47, 64
Proof printer **50**
Pulse rate 86
Punched card 4, **18**, **19**, 21, **59**, 62, **81**, 82, **103**, 104, **109**, 148
Punched tape 4, **19**, 21, **46**, **50**, 51, 80, **94**, 96, 137

Radar **15**, **78**, 79
Radiation 92
Radio-link 56, 58
Rainfall 83
Raw data 42
Read-only memory 152
Read/write head 60, 152
Real-time 40
Reed relay 123
Relay 37, 120
Renting computers 58
Reservation 52, **52**, **53**, 76
Resource scheduling 9, **10**
Respiration rate 86
Road junction 26
Rocket 15, **17**, 79
Rolling mill 113
Routing traffic 30–32

Satellite **12**, 16, 17, **78**, 79, **82**, 83
Scan program 42
Scheduling 6
Schmoo-chart 98, 99
Seat booking 52, 63
Sense-wire 97
Serial data 123
Serviceability of aircraft 71
Shears 113, 115, **117**
Silicon chips 140, 152, **153**, 154
Simulator 4
Software 5, 63
Space capsule 17
Steel works **112**, 113–116
Stock exchange 18
Stockbroking **19**
Stock keeping 18
Stock level 22
Stolen cars **128**, 130

Storage scope 62
Store 4, 109
capacity of 40
Stored-program system 121
Stores holding 18, **20**, 21
Strip mill 116, **118**
Sub-program 37
Supersonic aircraft 15
Supervisory system 86, **88**
Surgery 86
Switchgear 35
Symptom 92
Syntax 107

Table 42
Tape reader **5**
Technical library 102
Telegraph 51, 125
Telephone **18**, 22, 58, 84, **124**, 125
Telephone exchange 120, **121**
Teleprinter 4, **57**, 58, 123, 125
Teletype **19**, 21
Television **24**, 28, 56, **91**
Telex **122**, 125
Terminal, freight 144
Thin-film circuit 14
Time analysis 11
Time-sharing 58, 84, 135
Time signals 16
Timetable 52
Traffic control 24–32
Traffic lights 24, **24**, **25**, 26, **27**
Traffic routing 30–32
Transducer 37
Translation 105, **105**, **106**, 107
Travel agency 52, **55**, 58
Tumour location **90**, 91, **91**
Turbine 35, 42
TV games 154
Typeout **12**, 42, **97**, **117**
Typesetting **46**, 48, **49**, **50**, 51
Typewriter **23**, **34**, **36**, 47, 56, **61**, 62, 84, **105**, **122**, 123, 127, 130, 133, **135**, 150
speed of 127

Vehicle detection 26
Vehicle registration 130, **131**
Voice recognition systems **155**

Waveform analysis 88, **89**, 91
Weather forecasting **45**, 79–83
Wiring **94**, 95, 96, **96**
Word breaks 47

X-ray 84, **93**, 116
XY plotter **78**, 80